Regis Silva

Happy Colors, Happy Life!

ISBN: **978-0-6151-8066-3**

Text and Biography by
Chaz Reetz-Laiolo
Senior Editor
Northernpros Creations

Cover design: Regis Silva artwork
www.regissilva.com All Rights Reserved

Regis Silva
1977 - Brasil

The act of celebration lies at the heart of Brazilian artist Regis Silva's two- and three-dimensional work. By his hand we are led through a vivid and fragmented festival of abundance and famine, of love and prostitution, of life and death. Be it in his clean monochromes or his saturated multi-media pieces both the sublime and grotesque are always handled with equal reverence. Born in Paraiso, Brazil in 1977 Silva unknowingly embarked on his artistic career when, at the age of 16, he wandered into an art supply store and purchased a canvas and acrylic paints. Though he would continue his college studies and go on to work professionally in accounting, the seed had been planted. At the age of twenty-two he left Brazil for California where he began his artistic pursuits in earnest.

Inspired by the meandering northern coastline, its multitude of jellyfish and other sea creatures, Silva's seminal collection of oceanic abstractions came quickly. Colorful, mysterious and gravity defying, these studies display Silva's keen interest in his organic surroundings, but most importantly they introduce the complex dialectic characteristics of his future works. His bright pallet; his evocative cubist renderings of the face; and his obsession with the voluptuous, the sexual.

Silva's widely celebrated first solo exhibition at the Pacific Grove Arts Center, 2005, garnered feature-length pieces in both The Monterey Herald's Go! Magazine and the Monterey County Weekly. Other exhibitions have included group and solo shows at San Francisco's Blue Room Gallery, the Muckenthaler Cultural Center, the Pajaro Valley Art Center Gallery, and the Day of the Dead Celebration at the Museum of Art and History, Santa Cruz. However, it was the commission for the Hotel Des Arts suite in San Francisco that finally manifested the dexterous power of Silva's work. Having invited the artist, Bloum, to collaborate with him, Silva set out to rupture the static expectations of guest quarters by creating a space where one could relax and forget they were actually inside. No surface – save for the ceiling and floor – went untouched. No media unused. From mural to sculpture, fabric to acrylics, the suite exists as a joyous point of departure for the senses.

A five-time featured artist in BrasilBest magazine, the July 2007 cover piece, "Gossip", illustrates Silva's technical advancements. Where earlier attempts at the chaotic chatter of city streets fell short, this new canvas vibrates with the tightly orchestrated tonal exchange of multiple characters. But even more indicative of Silva's advancing artistic agility is his move to the three-dimensional, the sculptural. 2006 saw Silva leap from small-scale figurative sculptures to a crowning outdoor commission in Costa Rica, "Humanetee: The Tower of Life".

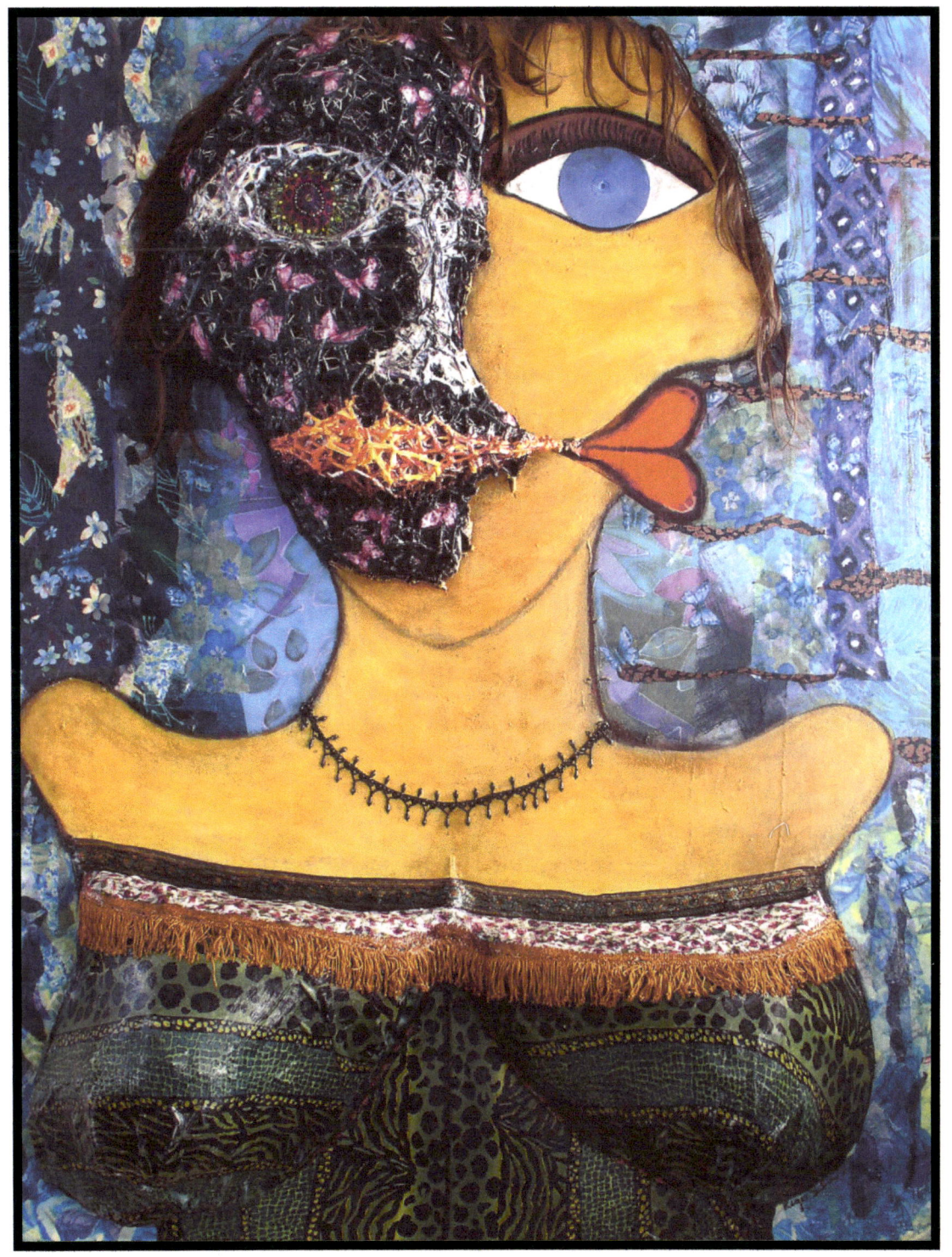

Mythology of the Body

To gain entrance into the work of Brazilian artist Regis Silva, it is important to first look back at the origins and wide-ranging influences of the Surrealist movement. A movement whose history is as full of the imaginative and unexpected turn, as the work of its founding practitioners. Artist like Arp, Ernst, de Chirico, and – maybe most interestingly in light of the discussion ahead –American artist Man Ray. Interesting because on the map, The World in the Time of the Surrealists, published in a 1929 issue of Varietes, America is conspicuously absent. All but an engorged Alaska seems to have been swallowed by the border between Labrador (Canada) and Mexique (Mexico). South America, save Perou, remains an unnamed blankness of land. It would seem, with both his native and adopted homes forsaken by the movement, an artist like Regis Silva might never come into being. But seventy years is a long corridor to travel and Surrealism has grown from Andre Breton's First Manifesto of Surrealism to influence not only its contemporaries, but a century forward into lands once dismissed and forgotten.

America, of course, would not only shortly find itself on the surrealist map, but at the very center, offering refuge to the exiled artists of war-torn Europe. The path to Brazil though would be a more circuitous one, traveling, some might say, posthumously.

This end of Surrealism has been appointed several dates but as is fitting for a movement of such liberating tones, it has refused its own obituaries. Some argue that World War II effectively disbanded the movement. Others would contend that the death of Andre Breton in 1966 marked the end of Surrealism as an organized movement. But organized or not, Surrealism continued to resurface with identifiable impact. Strands were (and continue to be) undeniable in film and theatre, Free Jazz, even the politics of the French revolt of 1968, in who's slogan "All power to the imagination" one can clearly hear the protests of Breton, of Dali and Magritte. A protest which eventually made landfall across the Atlantic in the Latin American literary tradition of Magic Realism - a very specific South American genre influenced by the blurring of realism and fantasy in Brazilian writer, Mario de Andrade's influential novel, Macunaima. And here, Brazil having been named on the map, one can almost imagine the artistic development of Regis Silva. Nourished in his schoolrooms by this rich tradition of storytelling, he will, at ten years of age, first see the image of Dali's, Geopolitical Child Watches the Birth of the New Man, which he'll carry with him leaving his Brazil for that once non-existent America.

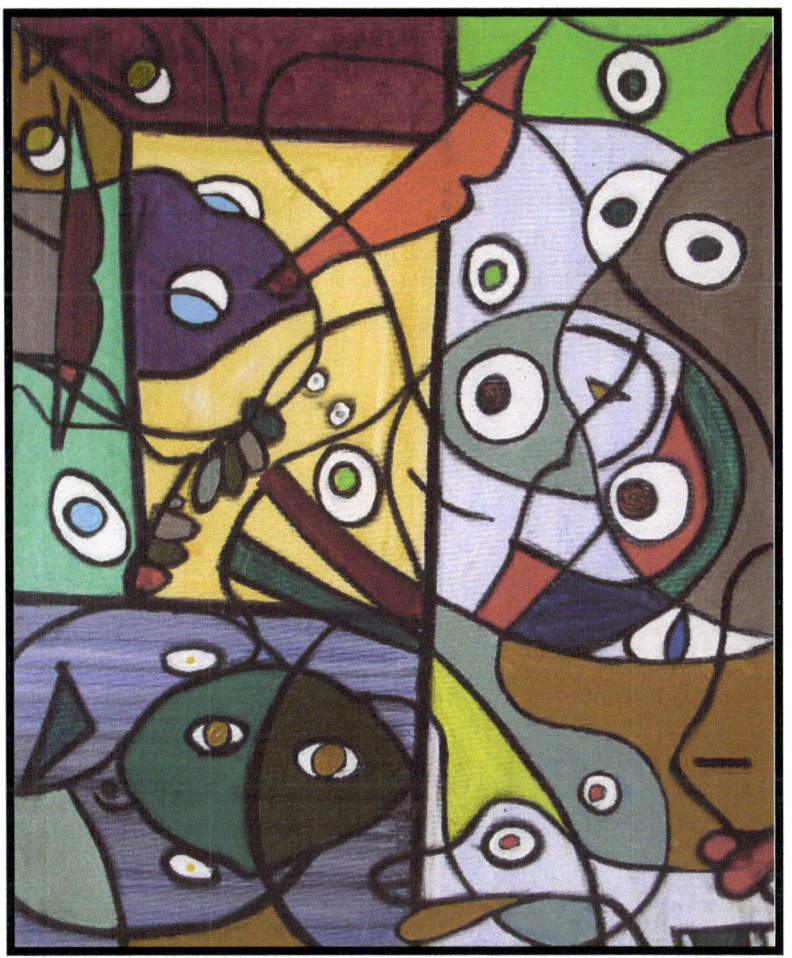

When speaking to Silva about this transition to the United States it is not his art work which he discusses first. "I had to adapt to a culture completely different from where I was coming from". The Bay Area, for all its exciting opportunities, was unrelentingly foreign in customs and language. Weather as well. So overrun by the tectonic changes, he didn't work on a single canvas for some time. Then came City People, his first painting in the United States. Colorful no doubt, but tame in its palette and size. Geometric, crowded. It establishes one thing with certainty: that Silva intends to free himself of the objective, the realist, boundaries of form in order to get at the roiling emotional core. His characters anxiously tumble without moorings. One seems to hoist itself up by finger hold so as to get a better view of the

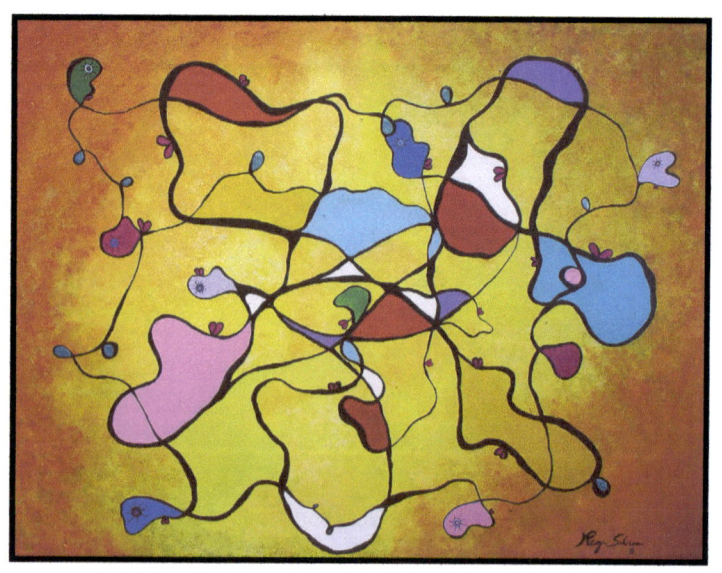

commotion, the goings on. But there is no rest in the piece. No native, no comforting, assurances.

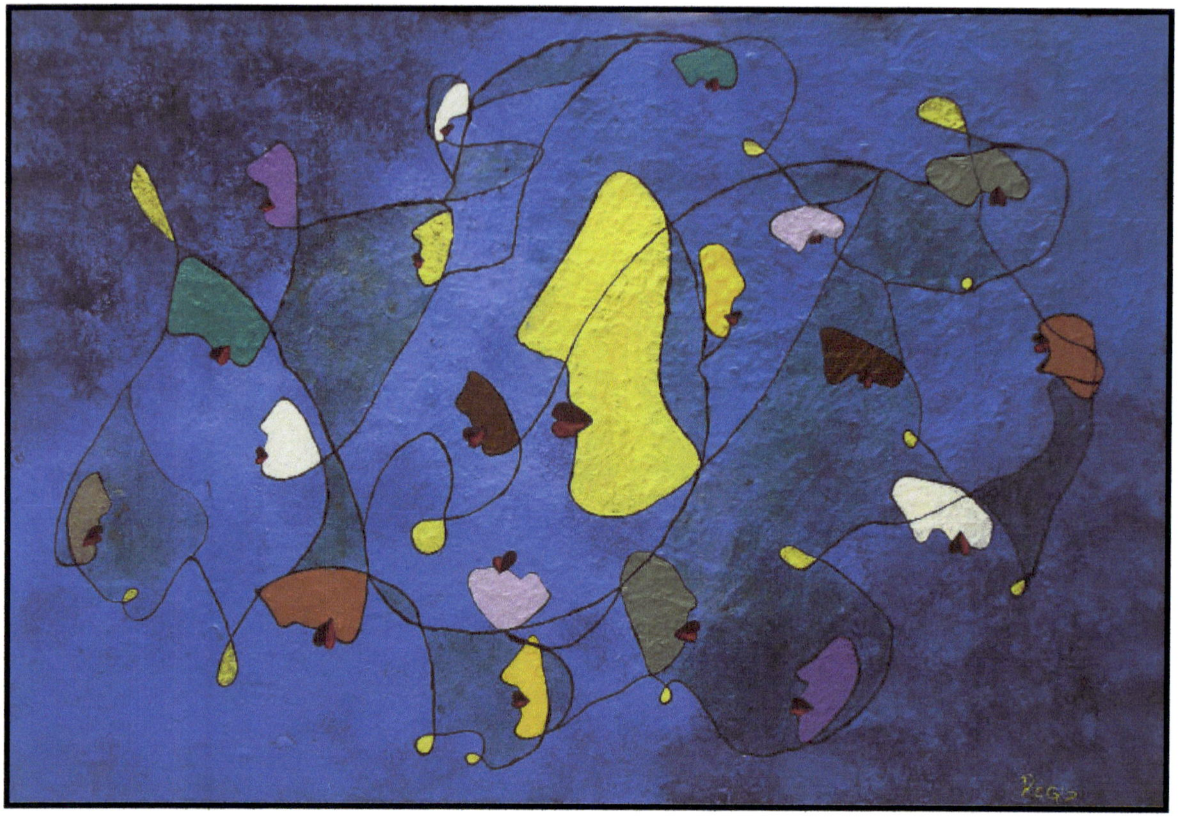

In what seems an almost direct response to the tumult of his assimilation, Silva retired for some eight months to the coastal towns of the Monterey Bay. Here his more celebratory work began.

Inspired by the meandering northern coastline and its abundance of sea animalia, Silva's explosive colors take hold in this seminal collection of oceanic abstractions. Vibrant, mysterious and gravity defying, these studies

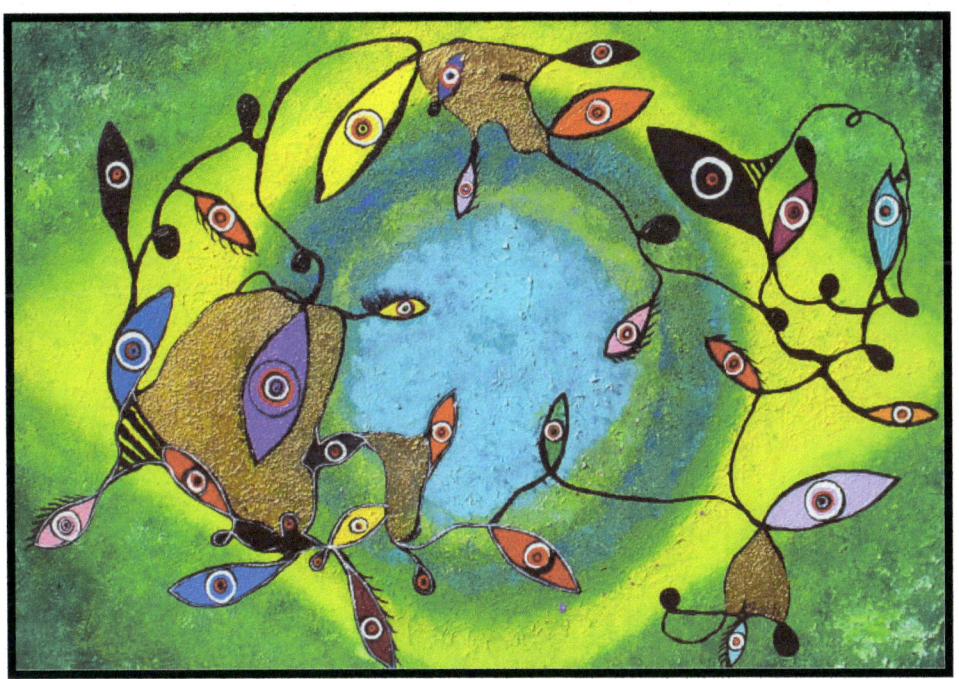

display Silva's keen interest in his organic surroundings, but most importantly they introduce the complex dialectic characteristics of his future works. His bright pallet; his evocative cubist renderings of the face; and his obsession with the voluptuous, the sexual. Furthermore, in these interlocking, loosely tied together ameba forms Silva begins to establish the importance of interrelatedness to his work. All is connected, he seems to be saying. No one, no action, exists in isolation. We are, he clearly illustrates, in this together – whether we like it or not. For example, in Brazil Eyes of Hunger, Silva sets out to demand viewership for the pandemic monopolization and waste of food products throughout the world. If we are all in this together, this piece asks, and can all see clearly these crops rotting in the silo, then why are some of us going hungry?

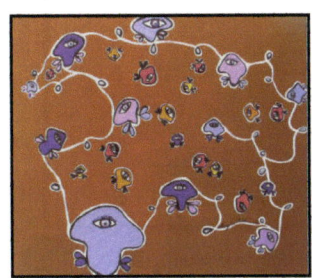
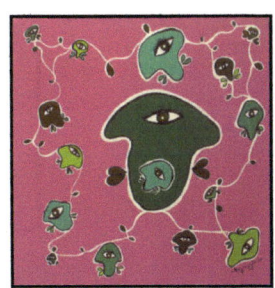
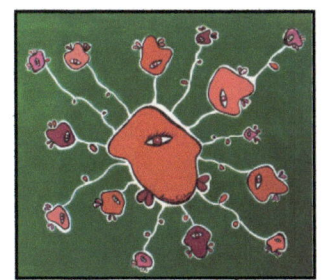

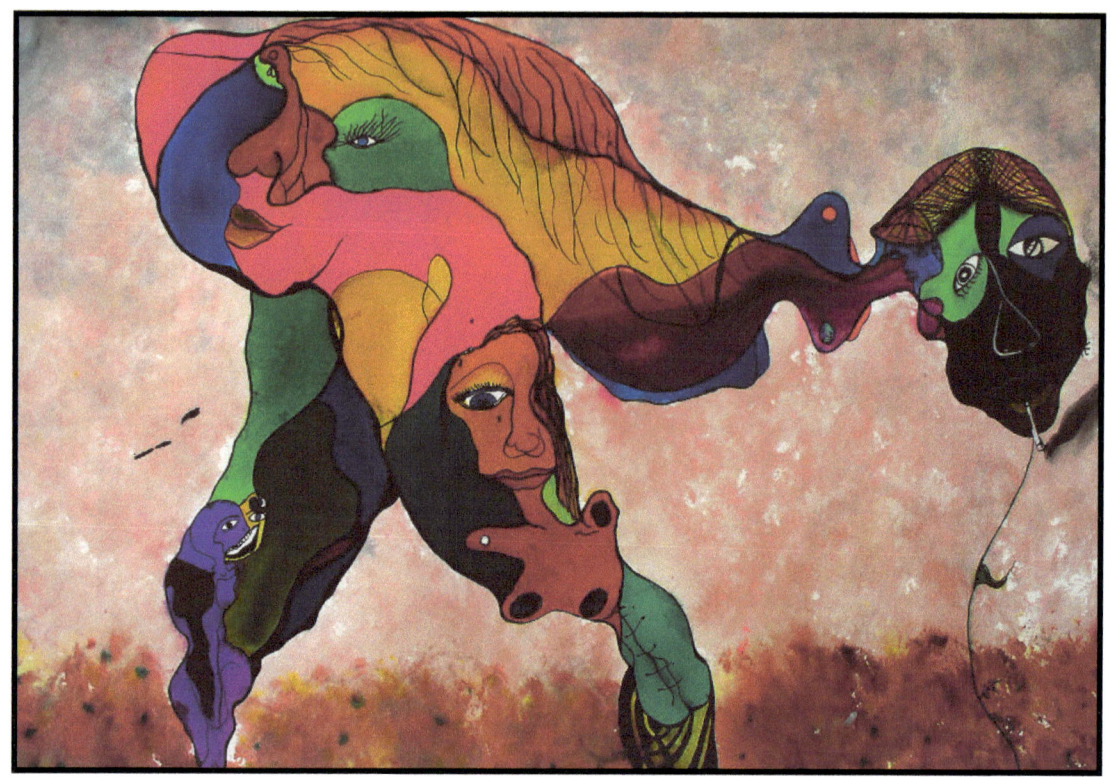

Silva's large collection of watercolors emerged upon his return to San Francisco. And in this new collection, his surrealist – or self-proclaimed Pop-Surrealist - tendencies come to the forefront. In line with the tenants of Surrealism, the works feature the element of surprise, unexpected juxtaposition and non sequitur. Their composition is reliant upon a peopled but barren, expansive depth of field. There is, in their fractured narratives, the return to order which was so central to post-war artists. But referential as Silva's watercolors appear, they are undoubtedly unique and completely his own. Where the Surrealists landscapes are mainly exteriors, vast wastelands

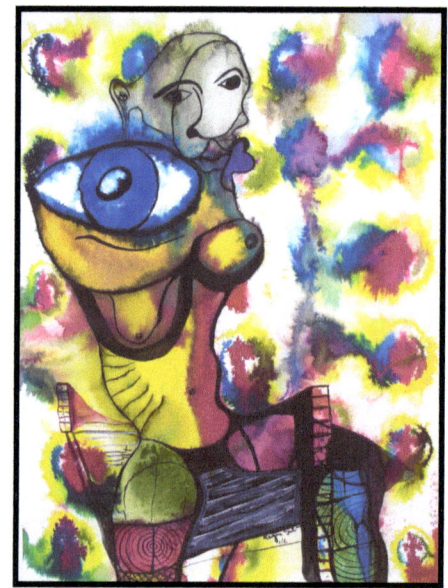

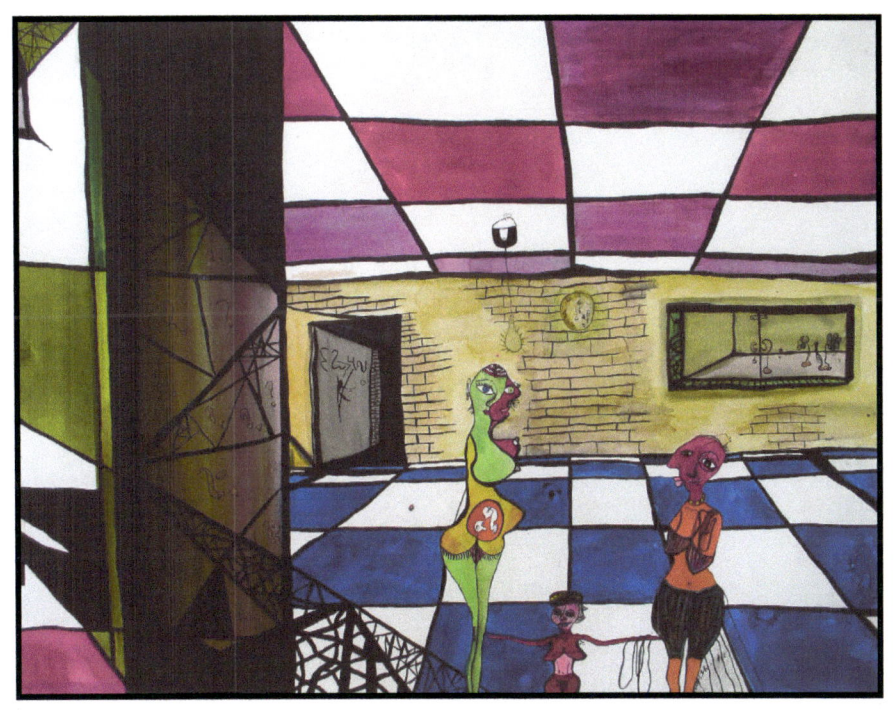

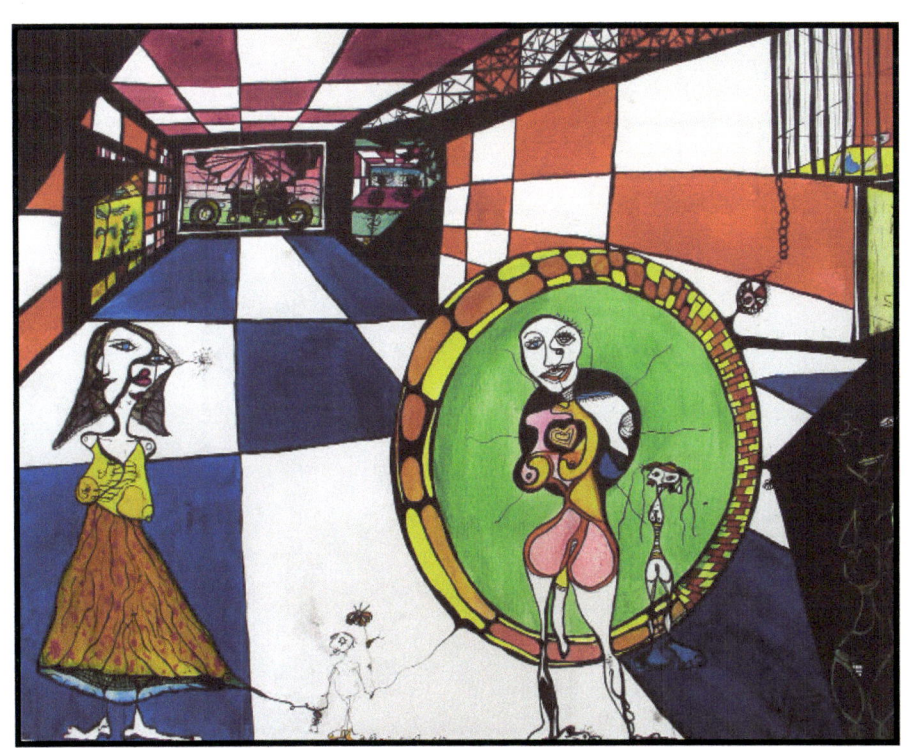

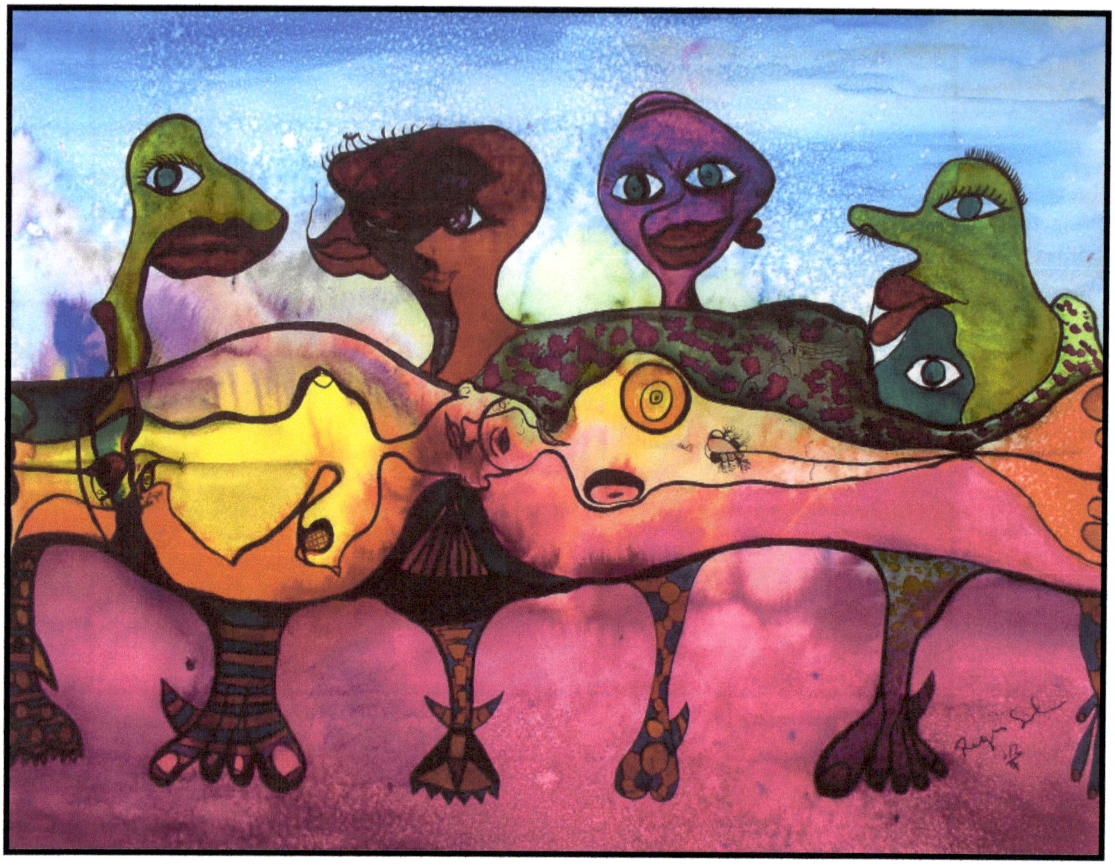

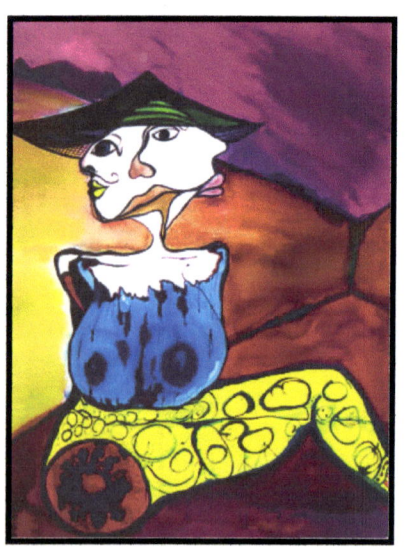
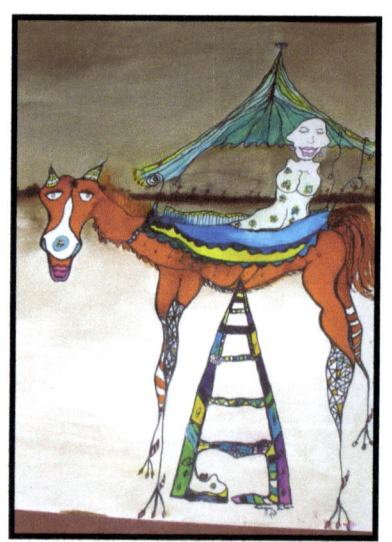
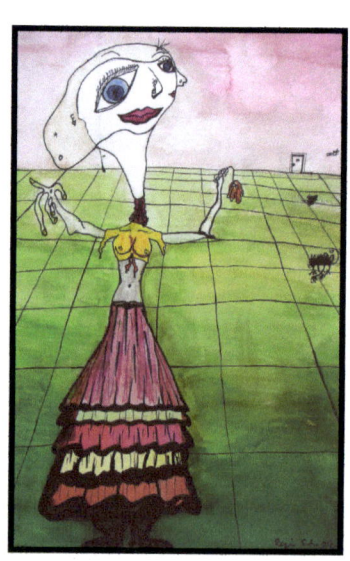

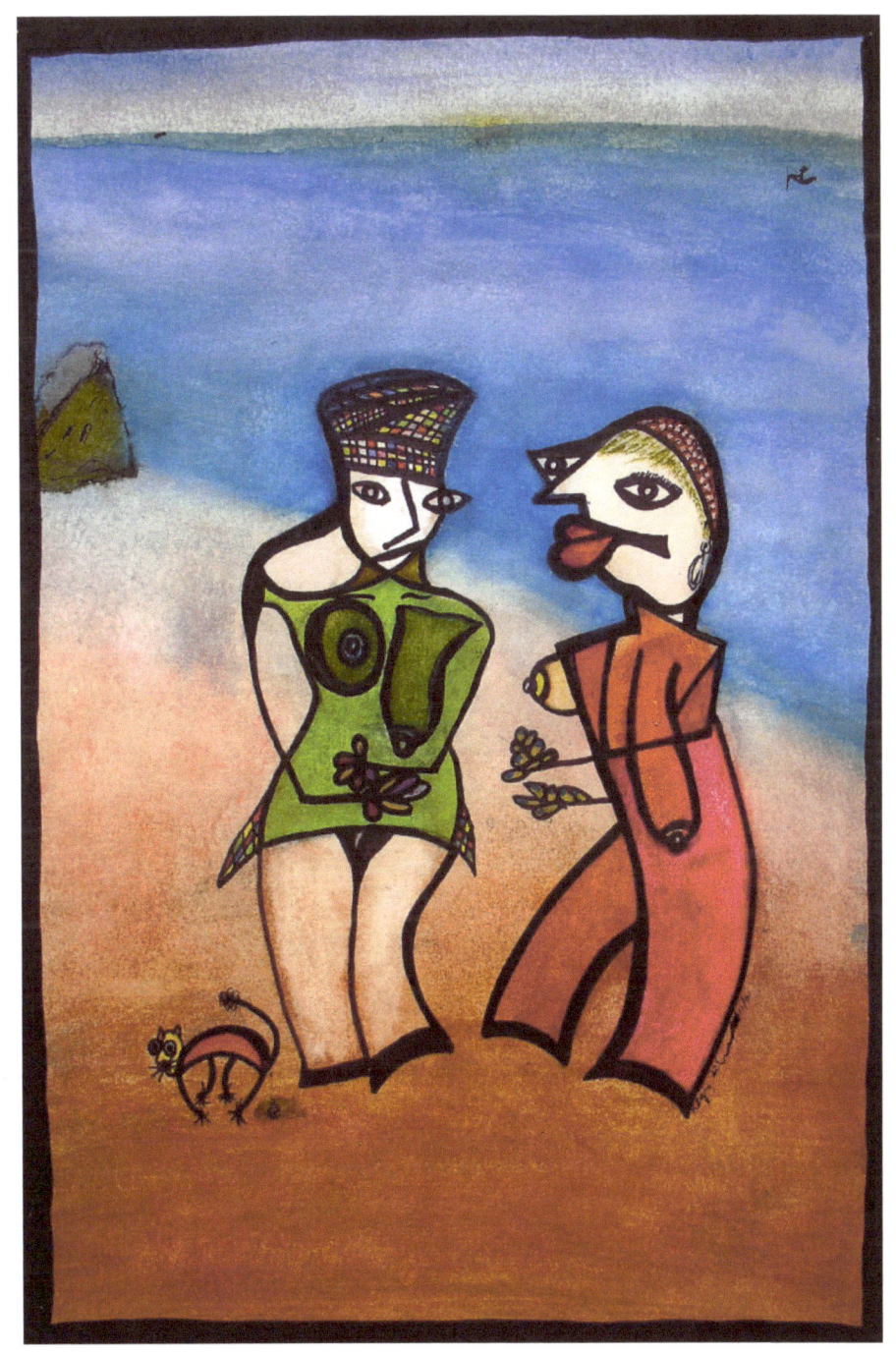

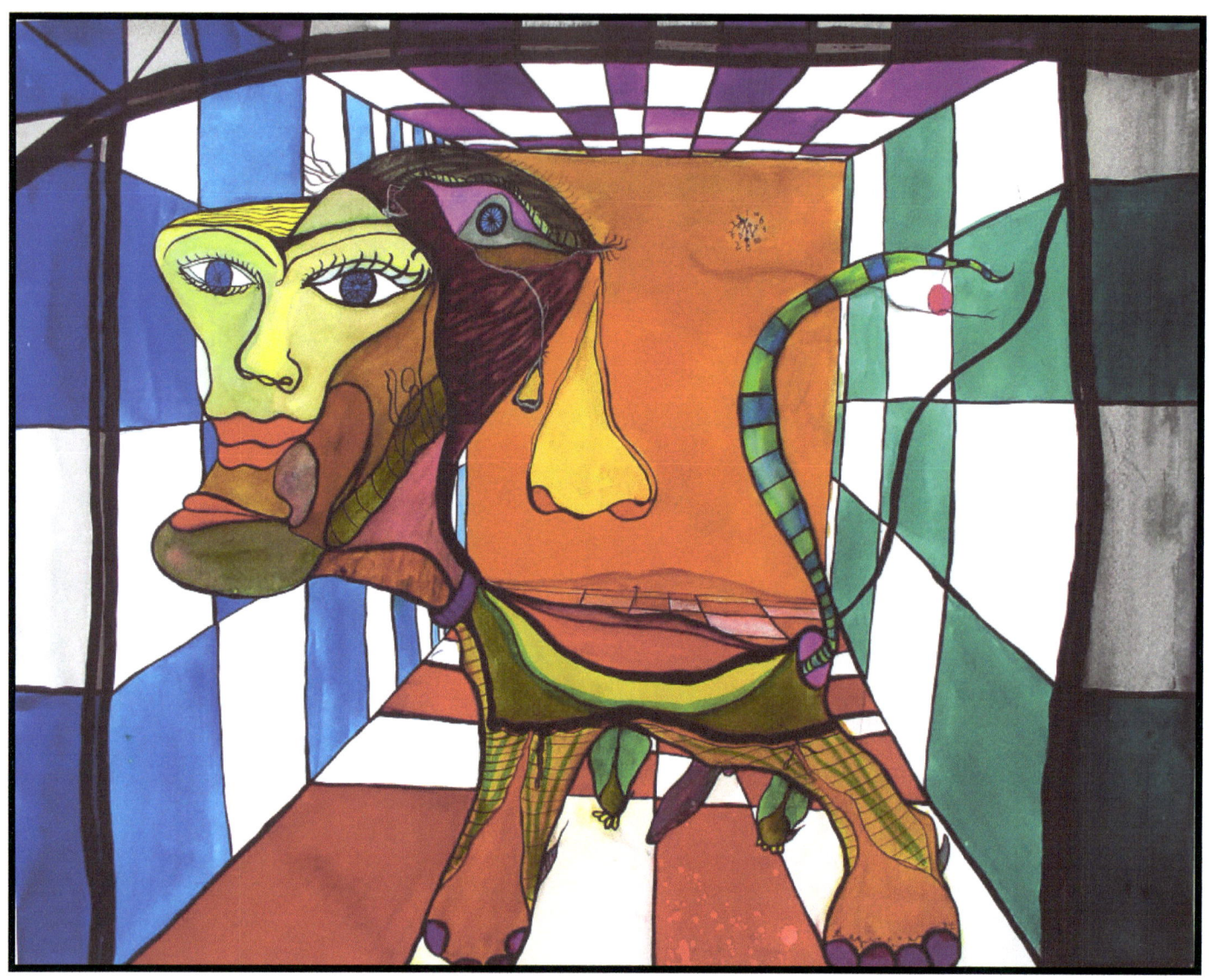

or subterranean voids, Silva's watercolors are predominantly built interiors. Checkered walls that narrow almost to a vanishing point, but never quite vanish, instead revealing the idol, the narrative focal point. How could they be anything but interiors when representing such intimacies as the artist's childhood memories and dreamscapes?

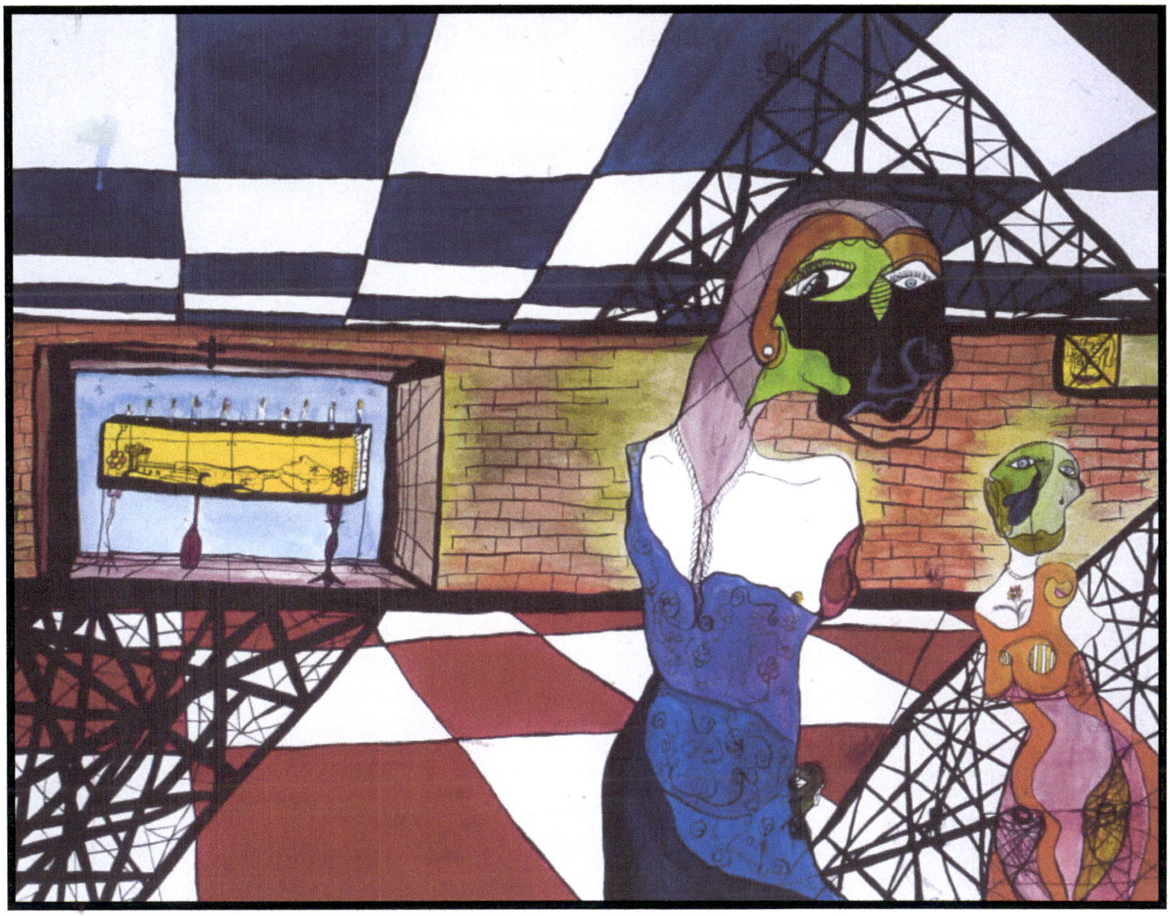

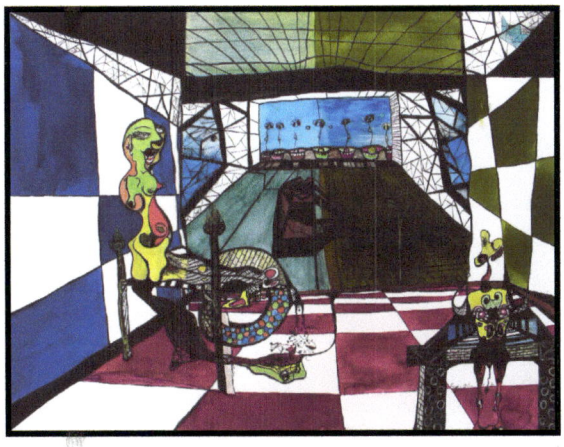

The Widow's Life is as an exemplary representative of this series. Two armless women mourn in the foreground, looking out towards the viewer as if to ask, What now? while in the distance a body lays in state. The women's costumes are colorful, though subdued by grief; odd non-structural girders occupy the space, but support nothing; and the checkered floor and ceiling recede from the canvas, drawing the eye to the casketed body. The depth, as is true of the entire series, is masterful. Each paint stroke accentuates the minute details hidden within the cracks of the previous layers, adding to the compositional depth with the illusion of live texture.

But these are only the physical demarcations. The emotive remains central to Silva's work. Through his gestural mark making and saturated color schemes he is able to convey the duality that anchors the series. The notion that daily life in Brazil is a coexistence of violence and innocence; of shame and joy; abundance and famine. Even while Silva describes the series as melancholic, there remains a celebratory aspect to near every piece. Be it in bright colors, or a secondary smiling glance from a character, the spirit, as in The Tearful Hug, rises from the apocalyptic.

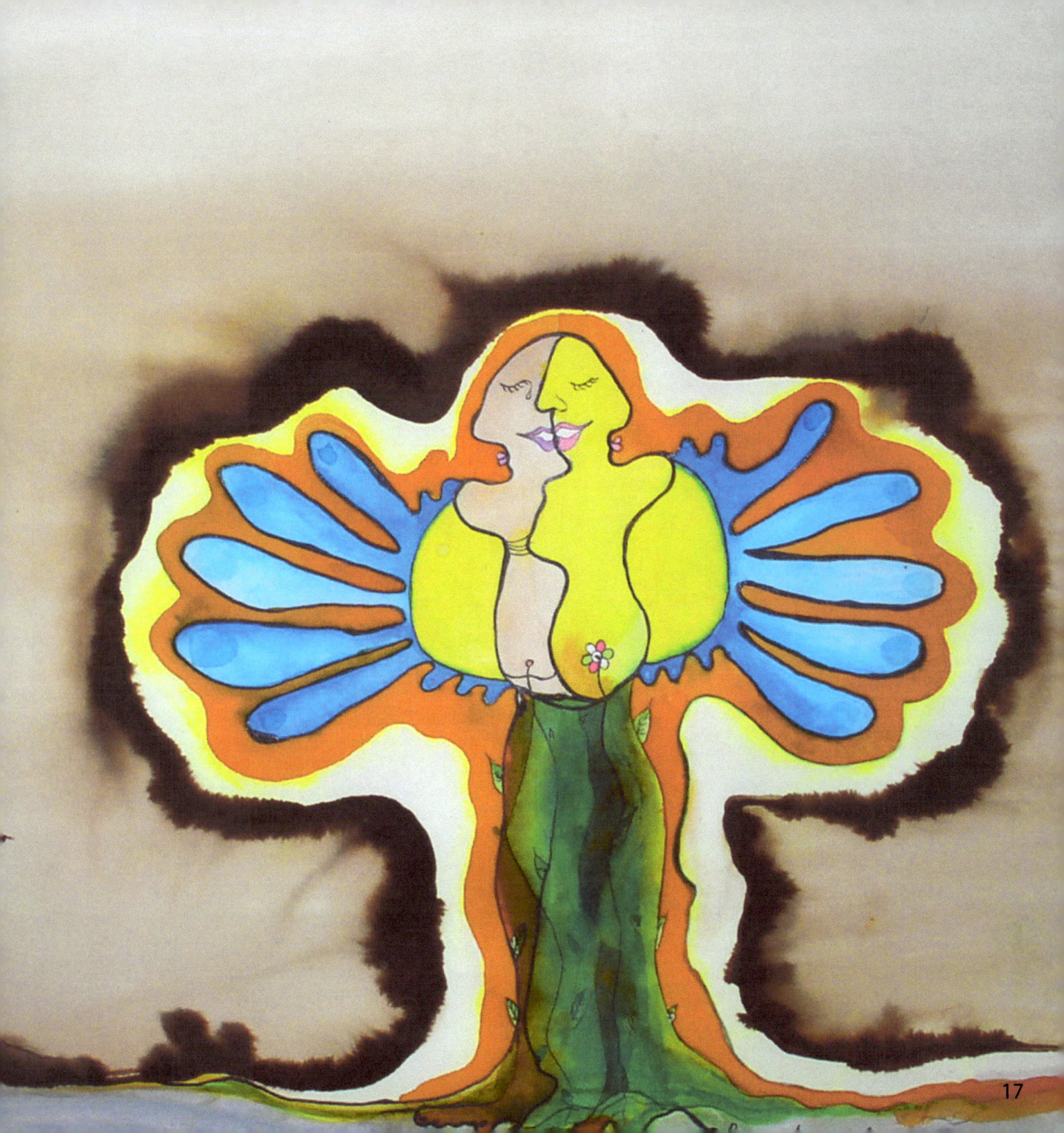

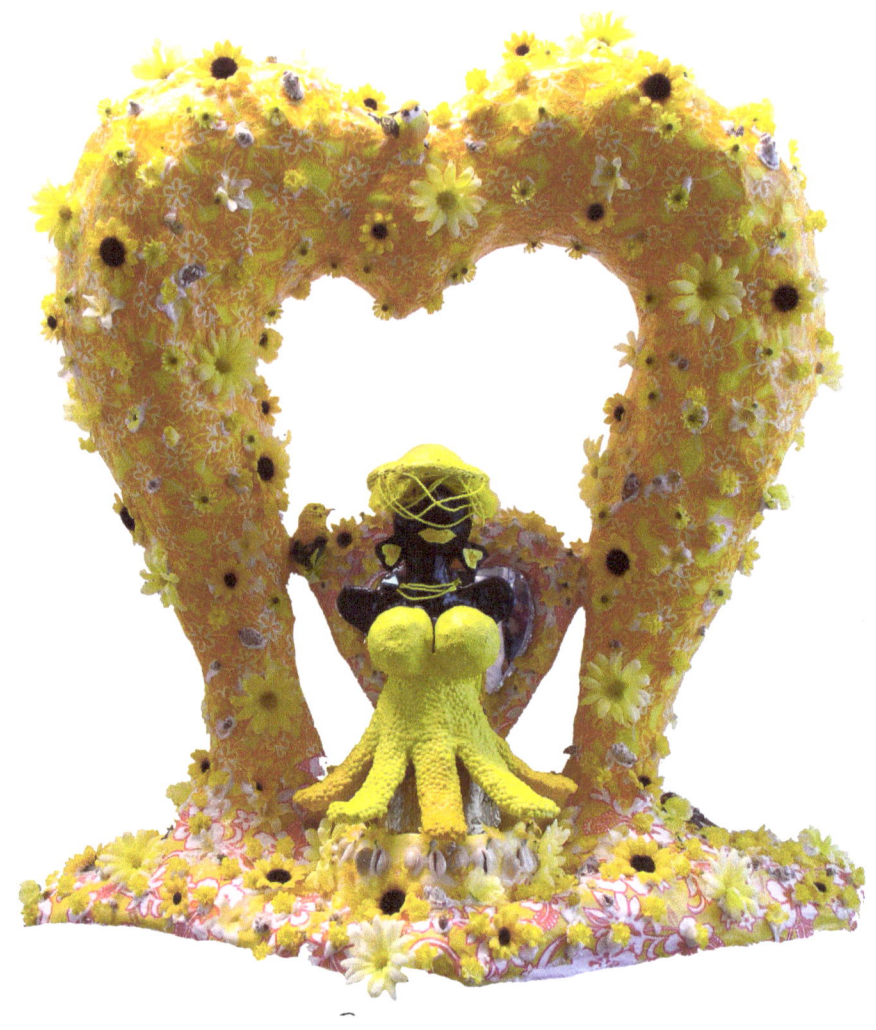

In 2002 Silva's research of the mythological Orixas would propel his work beyond the limitations of both the two-dimensional canvas and his own interior narratives. The Orixas, often referred to as Black Gods in Exile, were carried to Brazil in the oral histories of abducted slaves. Kings, queens, and mythical heroes, these African deities were worshipped in the songs and lore of slave encampments.

"The more I read, the more I liked about the whole mythology," Silva says. "It's a lot like Greek mythology." A mythology whose cross-cultural interpretations, natural animism and inter-woven mythology were the perfect accompaniment to Silva's own childhood fascination with Umbanda, an Afro-Brazilian religion.

In Brazil, as in Cuba with the Santería, African deities are cloaked in the stories of Catholic saints so that this forbidden religion may be practiced. So that its native voice is not extinguished.

"It mixes indigenous Brazilian, African and Catholicism," Silva says, "When I lived in Brazil, it was a part of the daily life. Many people go to both church and other spiritual centers. They see them as the same entities."

These entities, Gods of air and water, of mountains and animals, are among Silva's first sojourns into three-dimensional practice. They are small in scale when compared to the work to come, but no less powerful. In fact, these slight idols stand among the artist's most potent, most informed work, due to their rich historical context. They are Forces of Nature, each deity engendering a specific attribute: a color, a metal, a day of the week, a favorite dish, or certain drumbeat. Their colors resilient, their posture upright, proud in their bold costumes. They have, in story and now in form, survived five centuries in hiding.

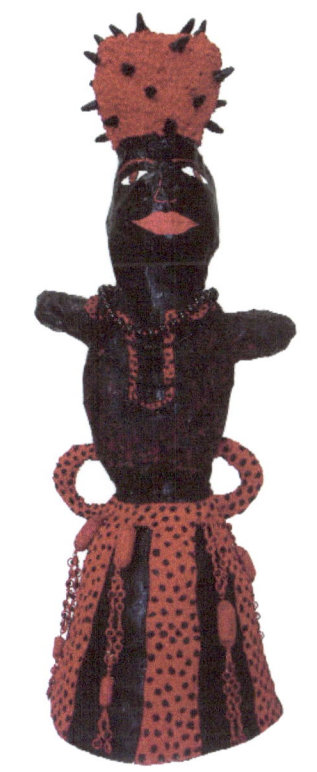

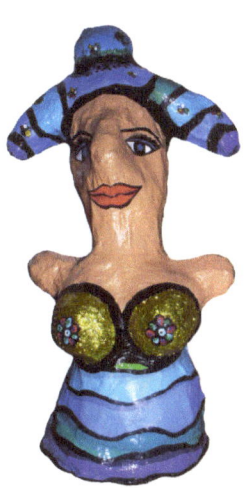

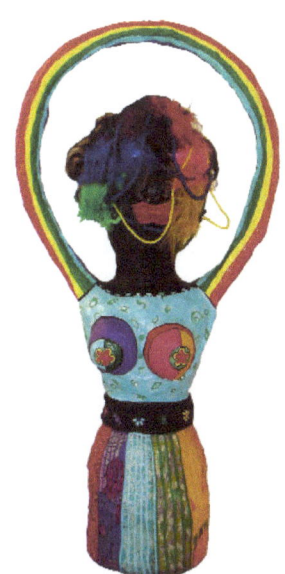

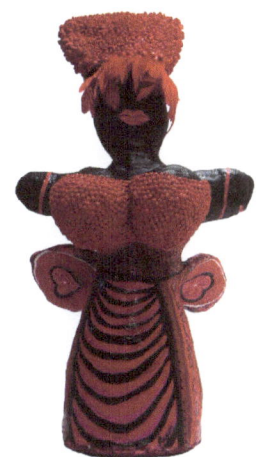

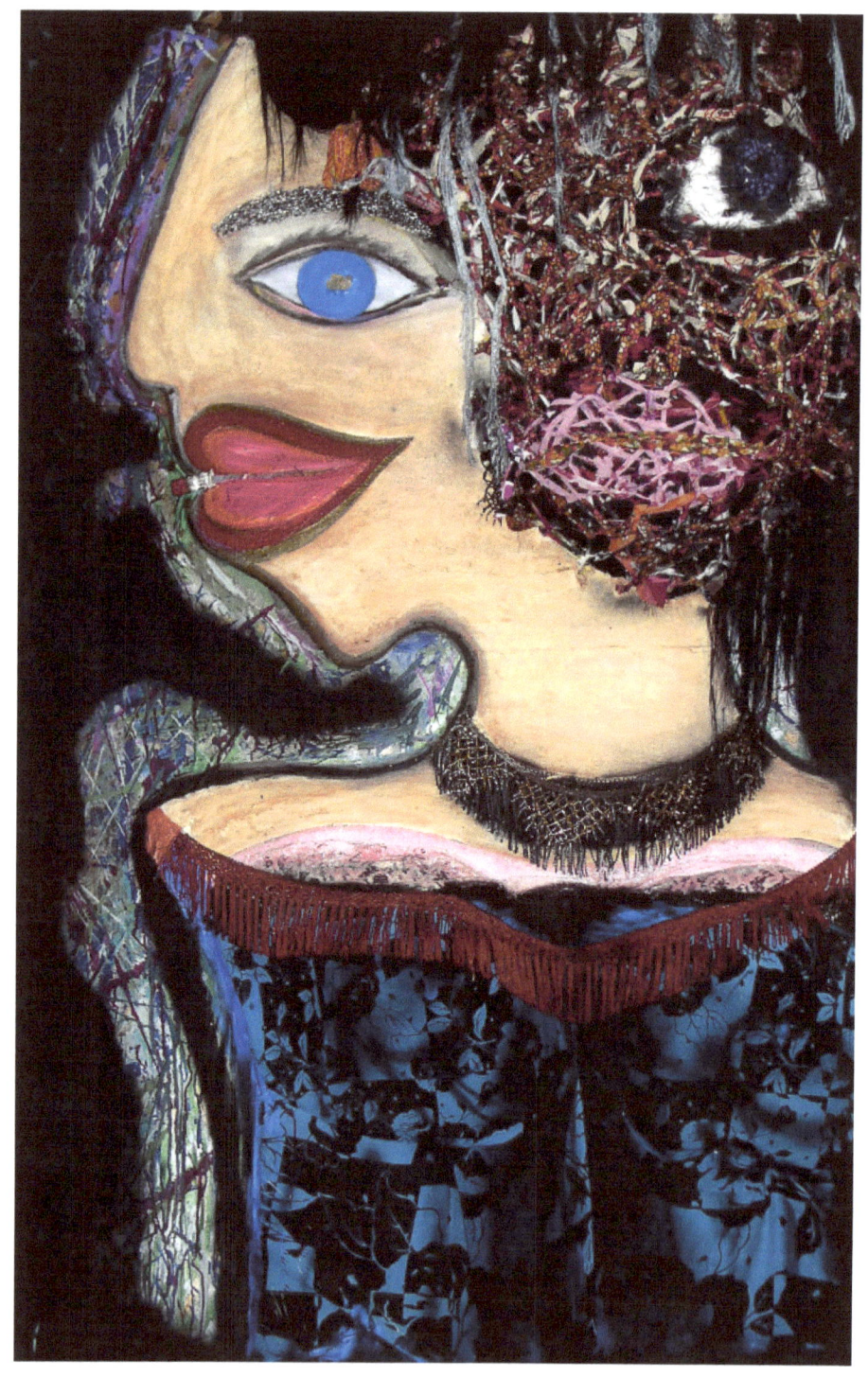

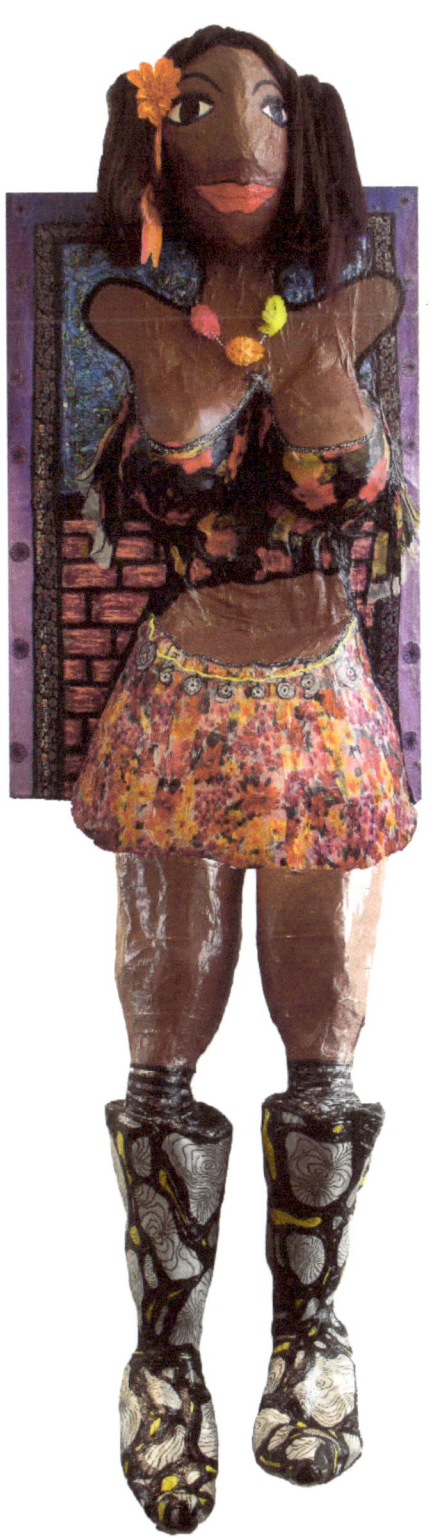

On the coattails of the previous year's Orixas series, 2003 would see the most drastic and lasting re-invention of approach for Silva. By exploding the combination of his painted and sculpted works he advanced directly into the body of two- and three-dimensional work that continues today. All as a result of one fateful step:

"I found a weekend garage sale in the city," Silva recounts. "A lady, who had been a fabric designer and was now retired, was selling fabrics from the '70s, '80s and early '90s. I didn't know what I was going to do with it, but I had to have it. I bought bags and bags of fabric."

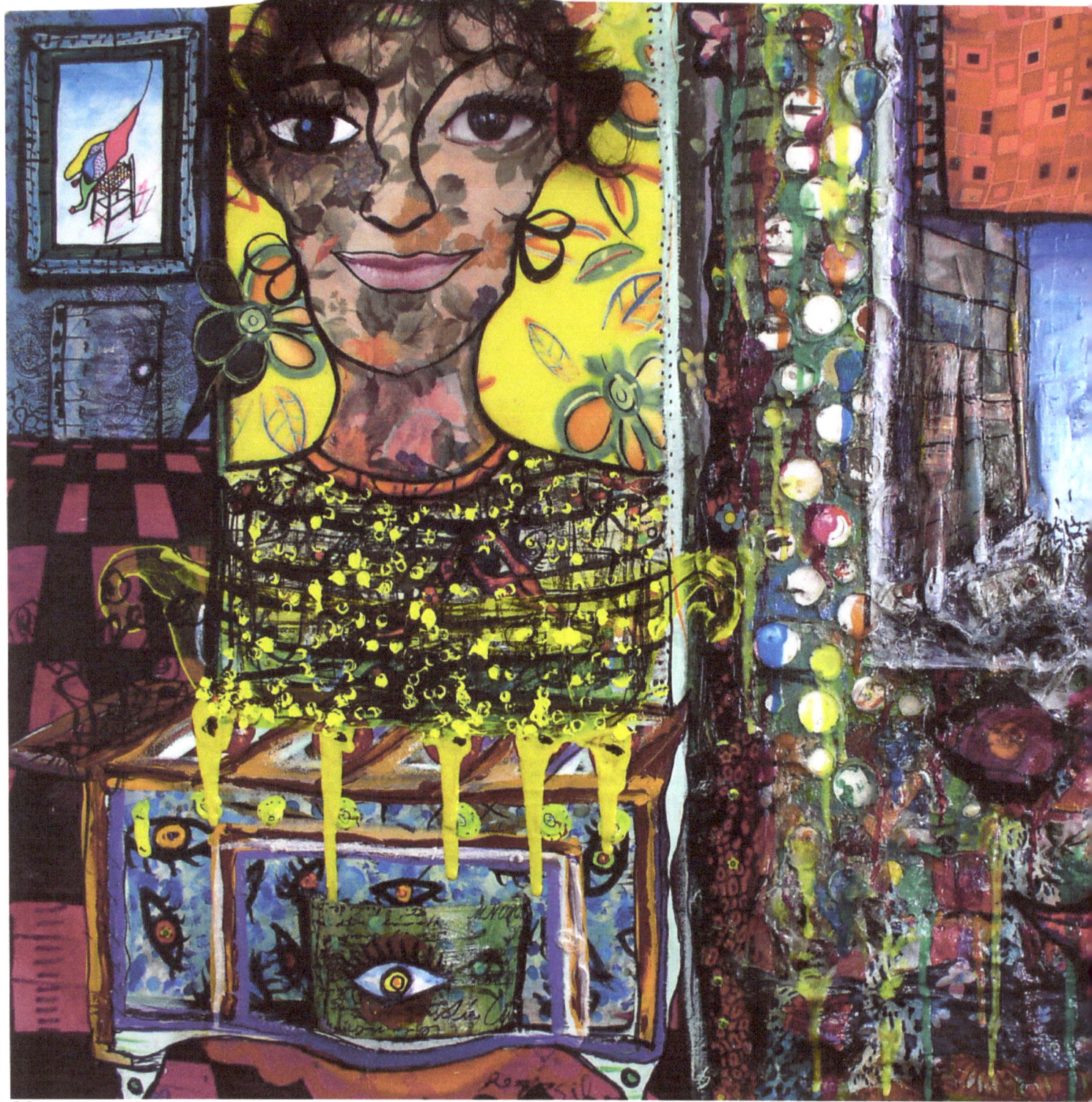

22

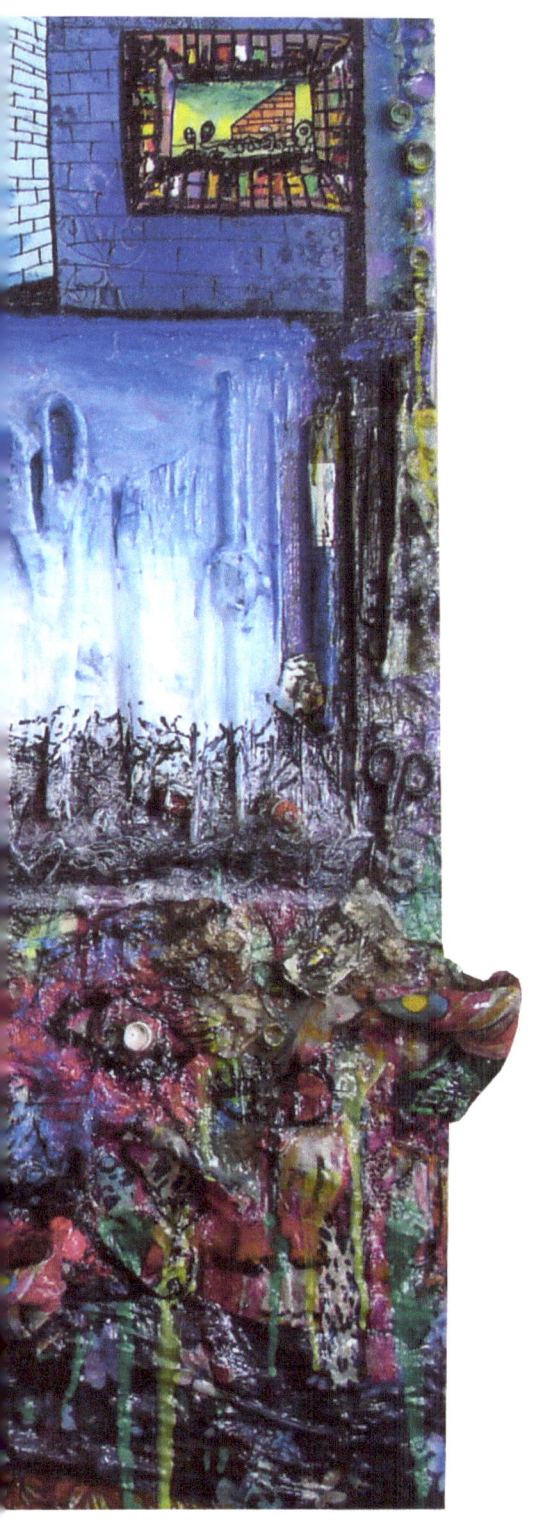

Fabric is the perfect media for an artist who of his own imagination re-rendered his departed homeland, his now receding childhood. Everything to this point had been manifested, created really out of thin air, in paint. But fabric offers the perfect bridge. Tactile, earthbound, recognizable, associative even, cloth anchors his otherwise loose, completely imagined compositions. For Silva it elicits the rich layering of memories tied to his mother's seamstress work, his sisters fabric shop in Paraiso. And to the viewer, it ensures comfort in the recognizable. It says, at bottom – This is a dress, on a woman. This is cloth, on a table you yourself might have gathered around with family. From there Silva's characters are free to morph, to float, to attend to physically impossible gestures and acts of magic in order to communicate that illusive impossibility, the internal.

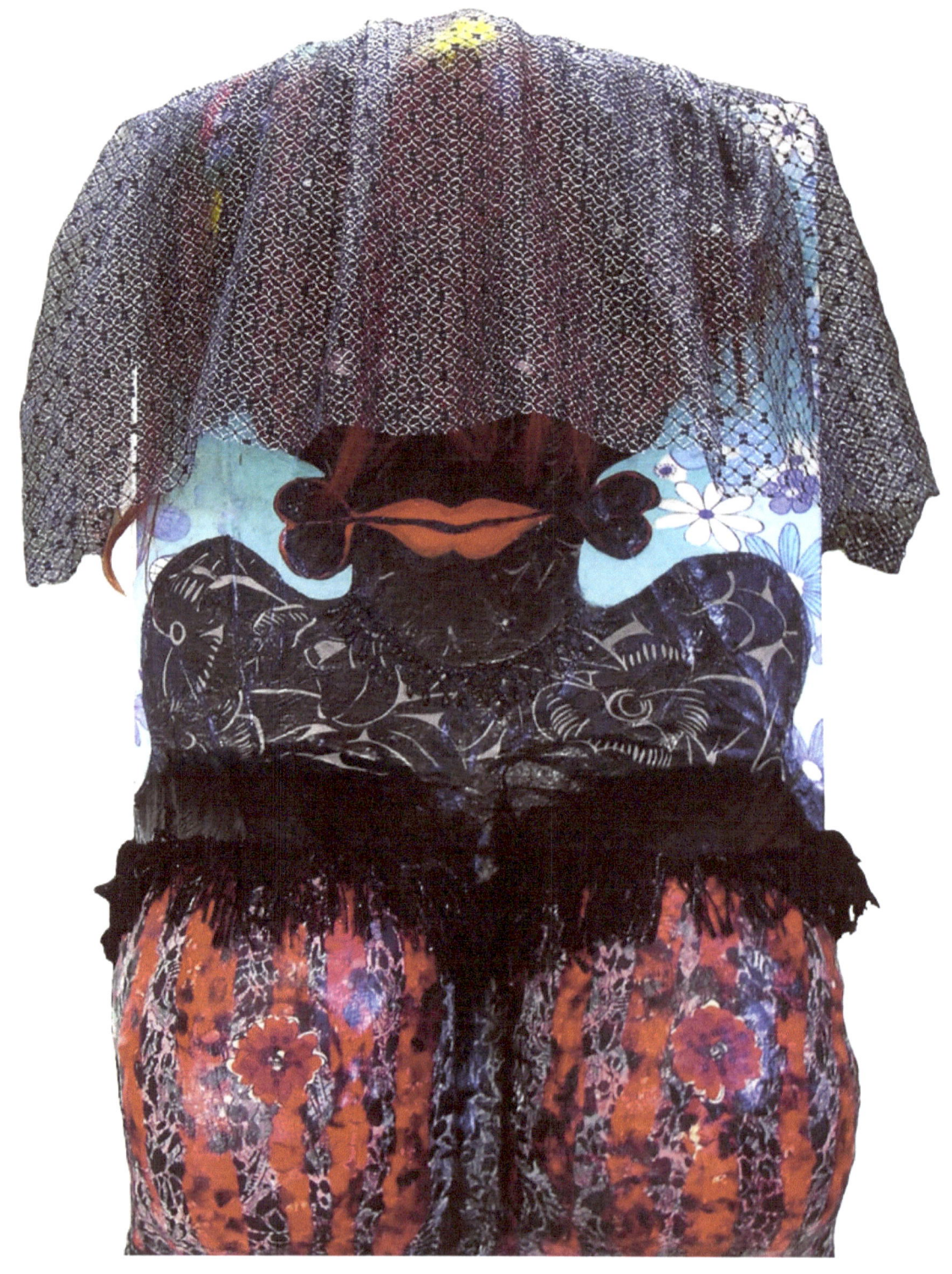

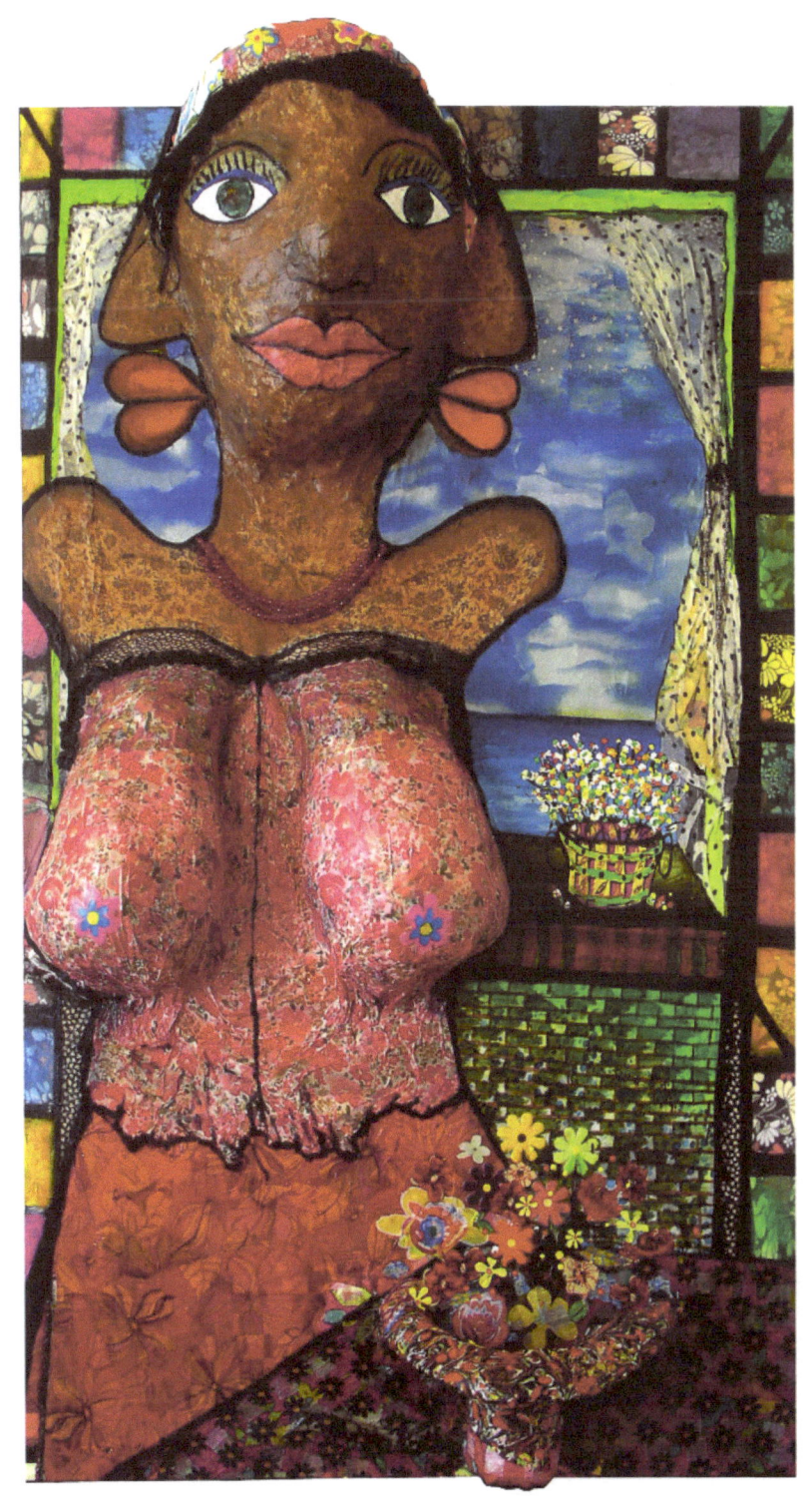

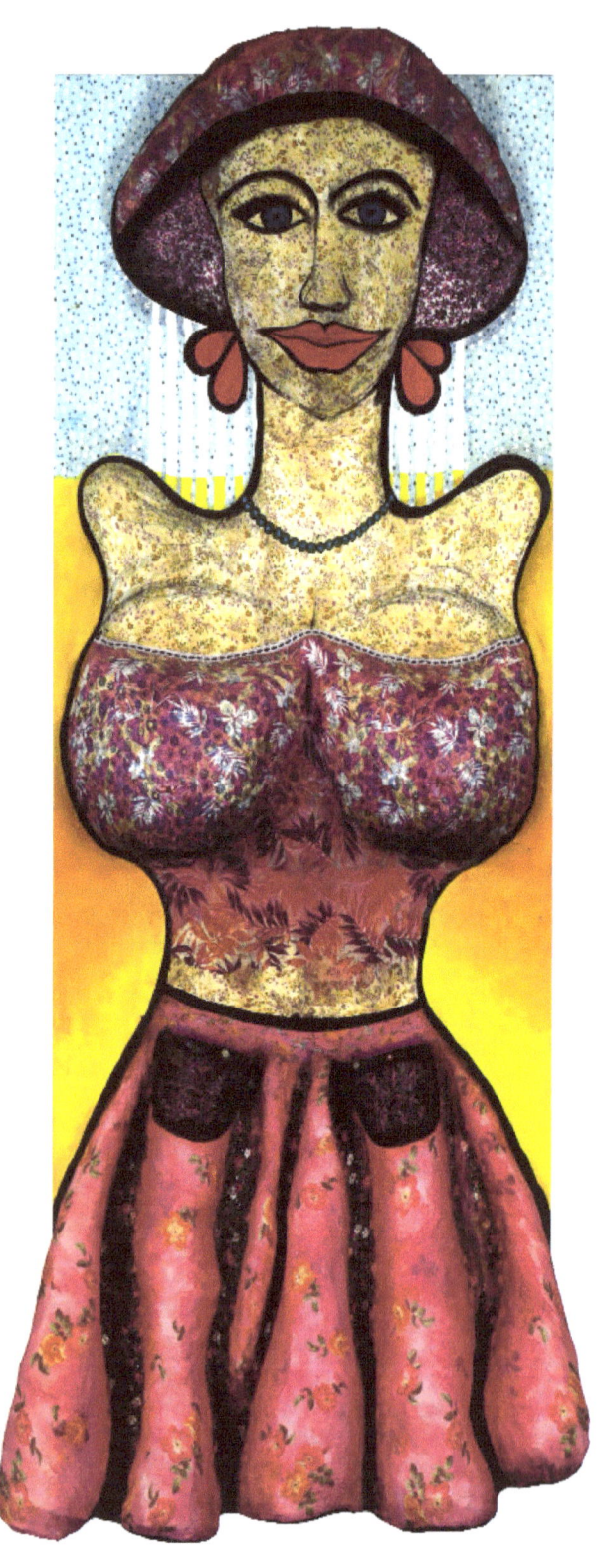

And with this new free-
dom, Silva celebrates
in exploding his scale.
Serena, for example,
stands 48"W x 124"H
inches. Her breasts ex-
tend thirteen inches
into the room.

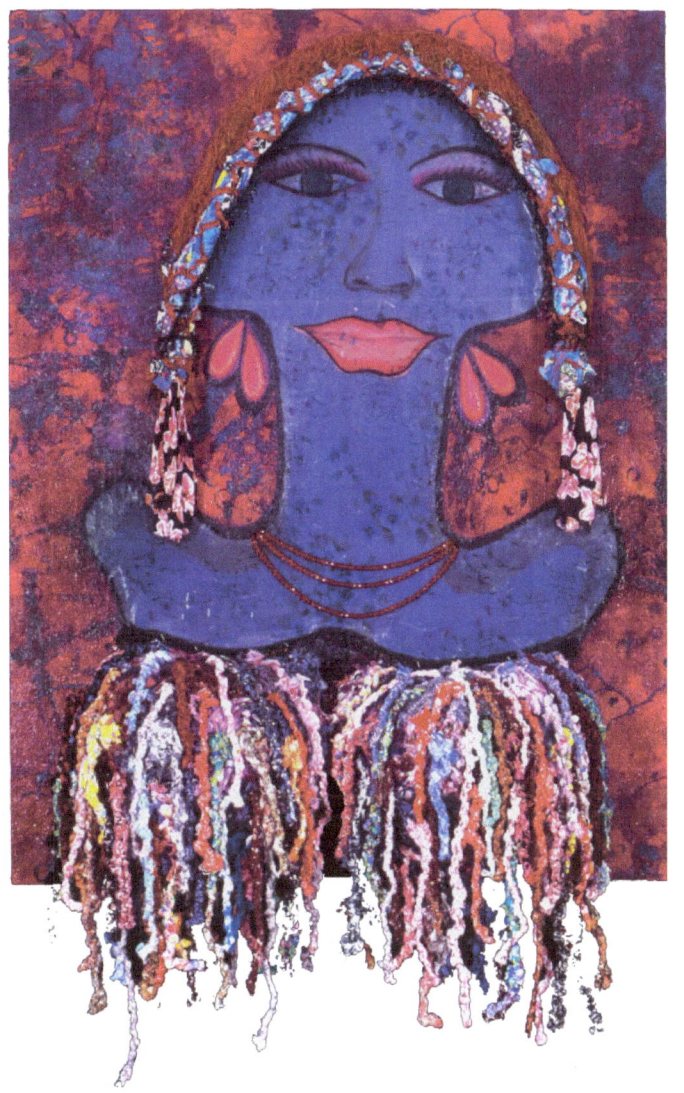

To realize these dramatic works is no simple physical feat, with much of the mark making and carpentry high up the ladder's back. To anchor the weight of the piece Silva starts with a wooden panel wrapped in canvas. From there he begins three-dimensionalizing, building out the skeleton with recyclable materials such as newspaper, magazines and bottles. Wire, metal and nails are used only for support. Once this sub-structure is in place, it is covered in canvas and sealed. Then, as Silva says, the best part begins. The painting, and the birth of his characters.

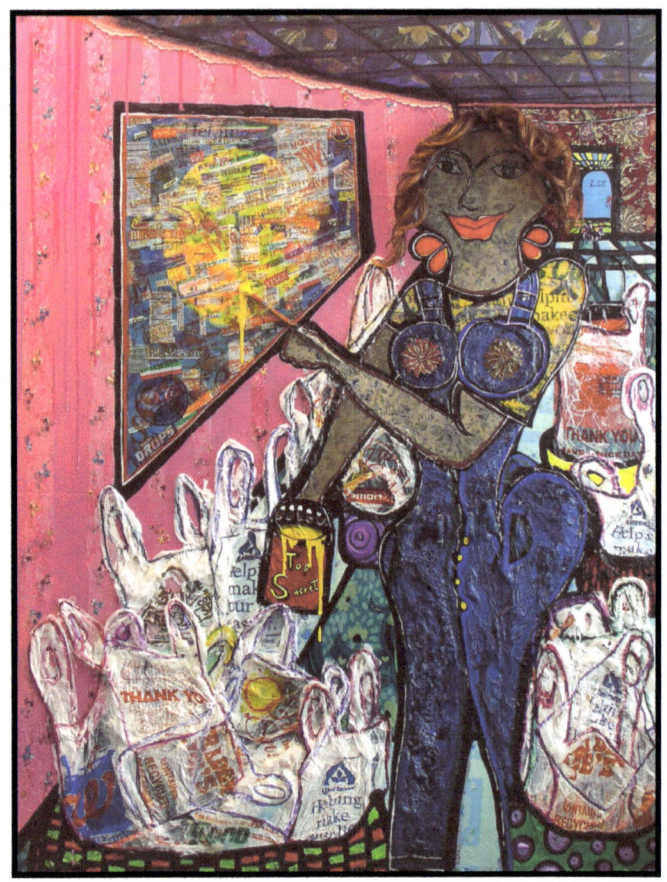

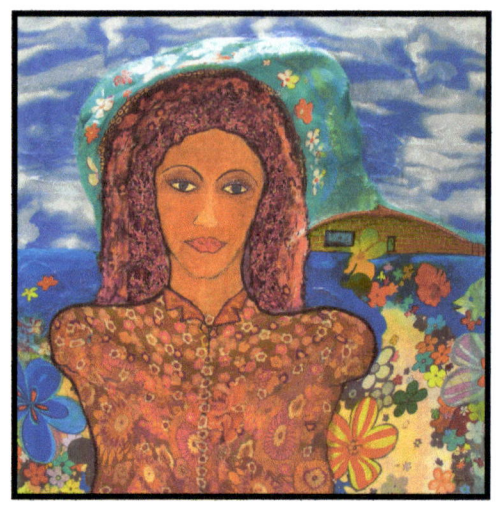

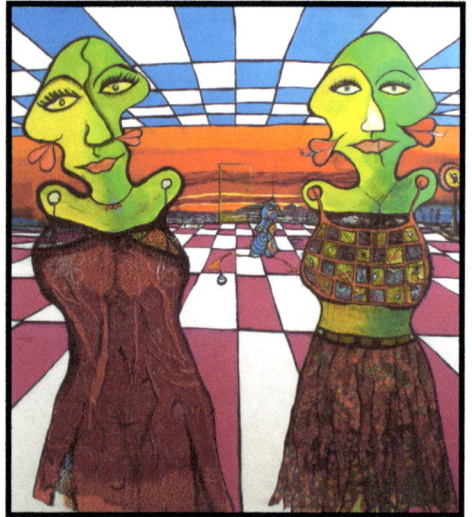

Their bodies (primarily female) are central to this series. And though the body has been sexualized in Silva's work to this point, it has not appeared as it does in this first fabric-ed series, a series that will go on, in 2005, to make up the artist's first solo exhibition, The Beauty and the Trash, at the Pacific Grove Arts Center. In keeping with the early abstractions and misshapen bodies of the watercolor series, nearly all the characters remain armless with dualistic faces. However, they are otherwise proportionate, colloquial even, except for their central feature, greatly oversized breasts, which, though now clothed, heave three-dimensionally from the canvas. Breasts which not only interrupt the space, but command the narrative of each piece. Veiled in mourning in one case; exploding with confetti in another; and

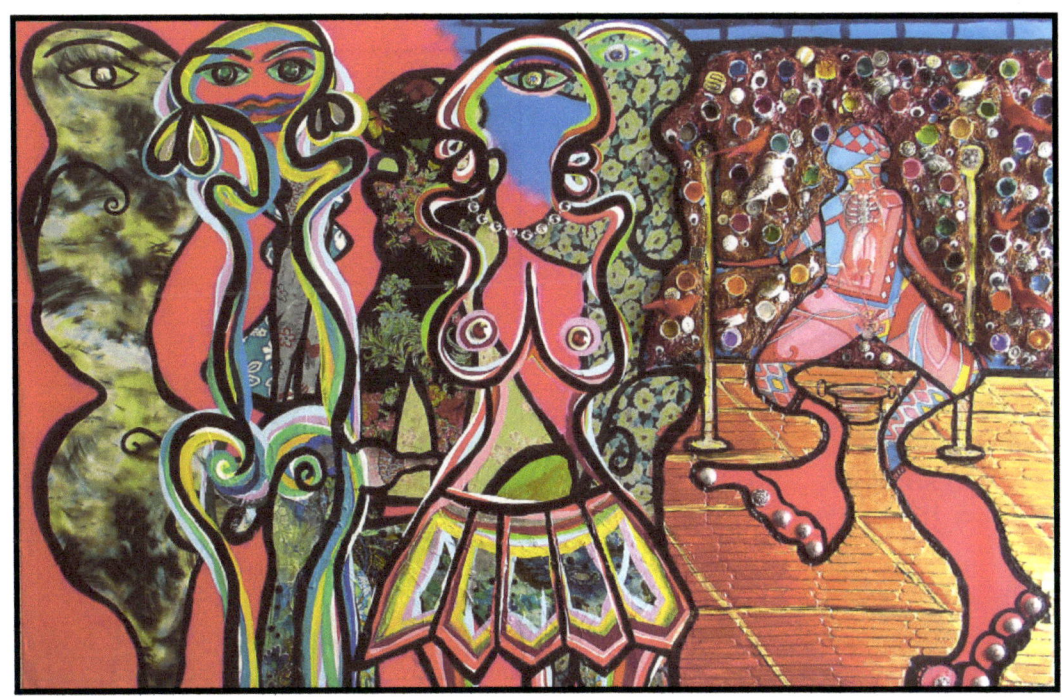

finally, den to a pair of snakes whose venom tells the truth of an otherwise bright and inviting work.

Inside these folkish compositions, of wallpapered interiors often adorned with bouquets, the question begs attention: are these female characters the Prostitute, or the Mother figure returned to the artist through fabric? Or, are they simply Silva's Brazil.

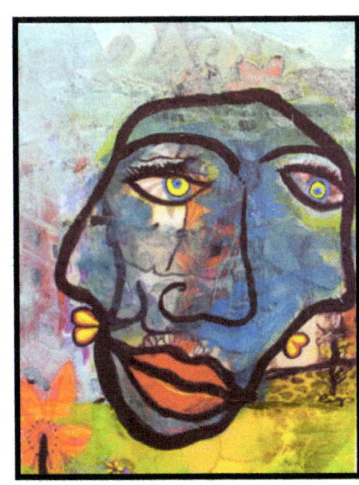

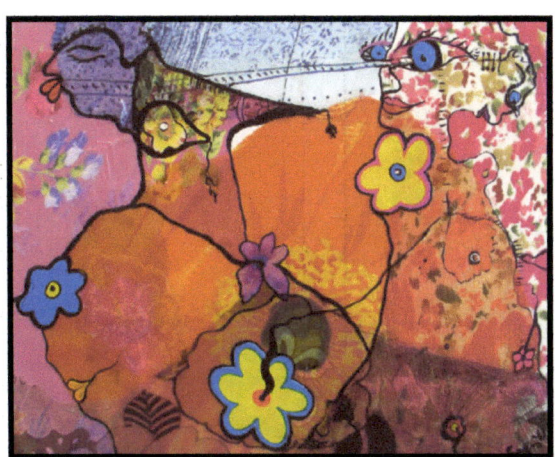

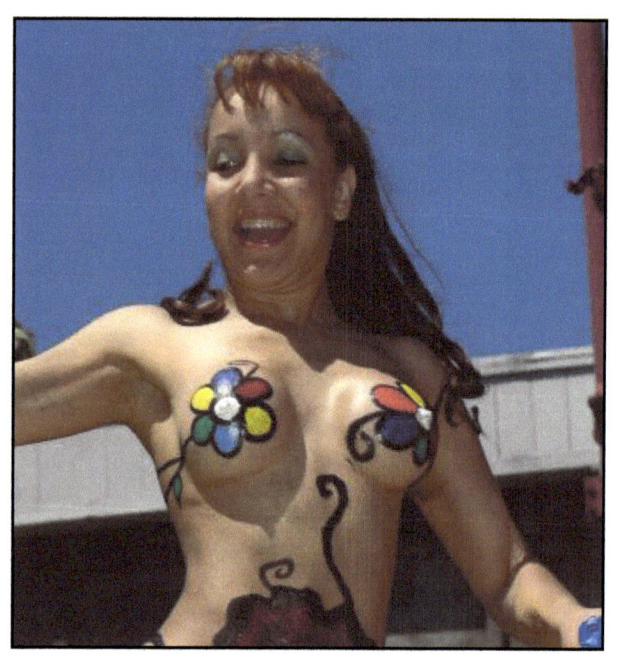

$2$005 would prove to be a very busy year for Silva. First, his solo exhibition, The Beauty and the Trash. And secondly, a new small-scale series of amorous sculptures. To accompany the exhibited work in The Beauty and the Trash, Silva decided to explore yet another avenue for his textile work, by returning fabric to its utilitarian roots in clothing. It is fitting with the previous developments of his work: first his dedication to the boundaried realm of painting, which then through the Orixa myths and finally with the inherent desires of fabric to be three-dimensionalized, he began to work away from the canvas. To widen his practice. Even painting

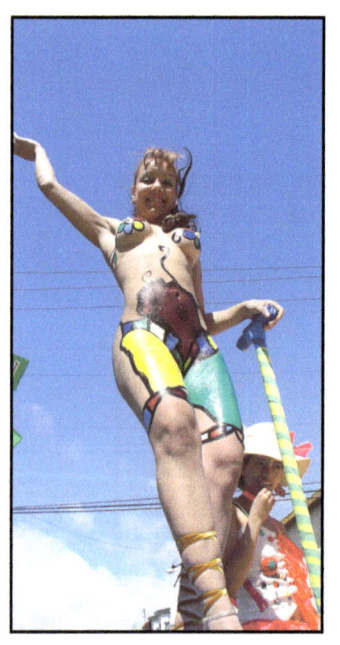
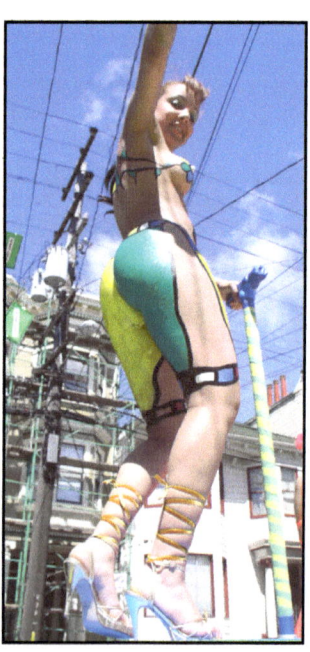
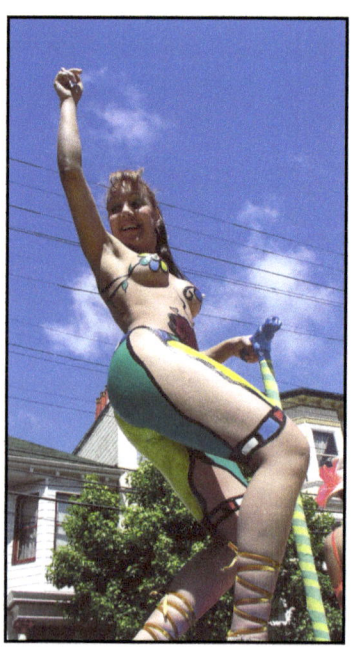
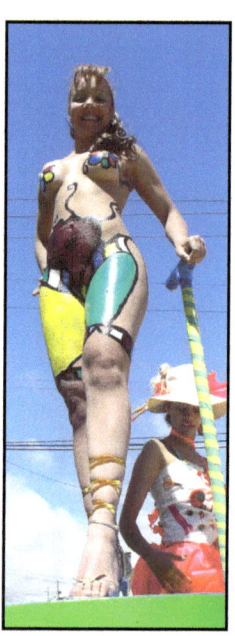

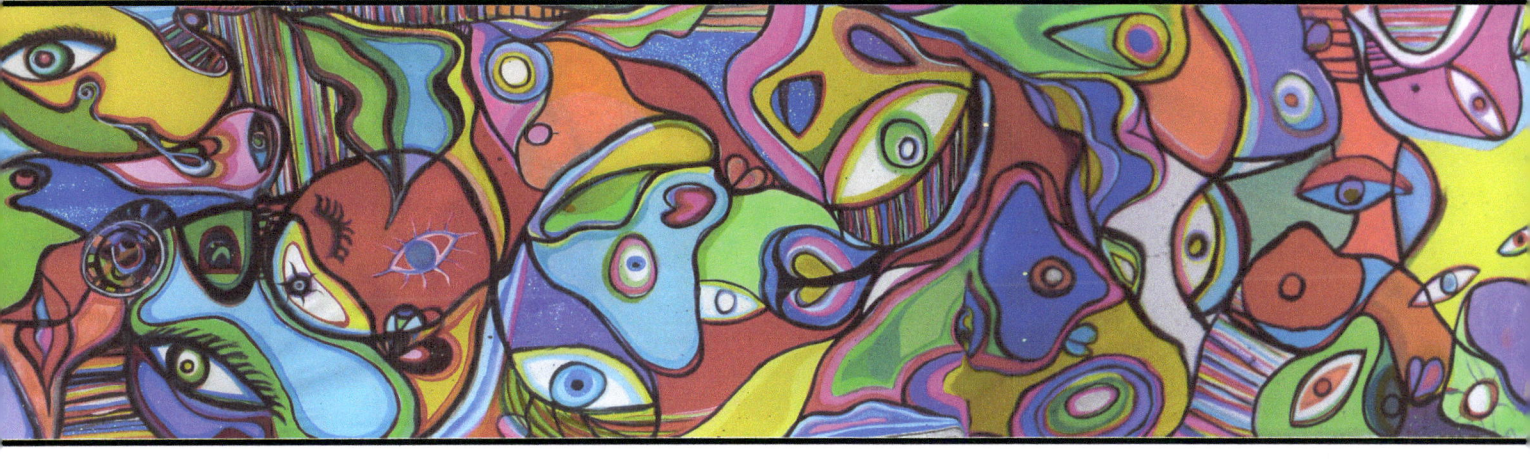

on skin – he would clothe a dancer in his brushstrokes for a float in San Francisco's own Carnival. And then, upon the wild response for this first fully integrated three-dimensional painting, he choose again the grounded and beautiful human form to illuminate his exhibit. To walk among them, emerge from them, sing with their voices. The dramatic ten-foot fabric mural worn by Brazilian Bossa Nova singer, Dandara, is in many ways the perfect link between the early and future works of the Artist.

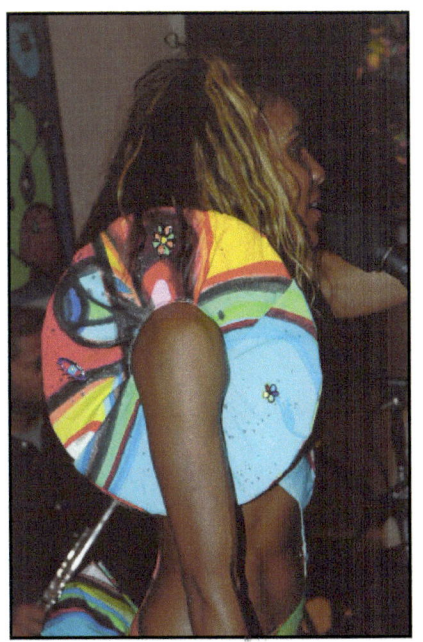
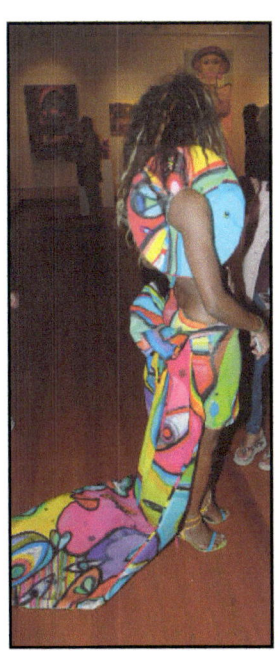
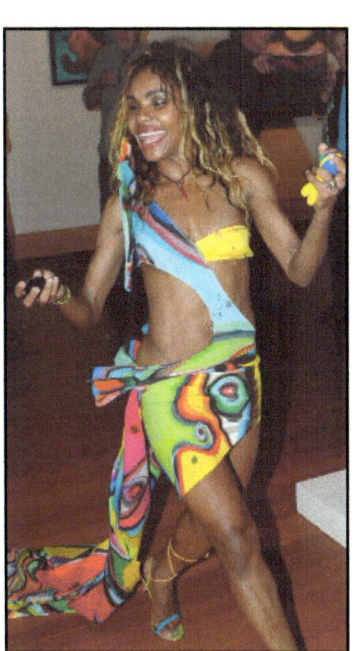
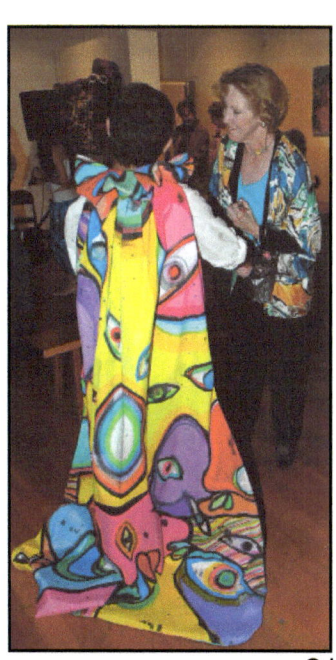

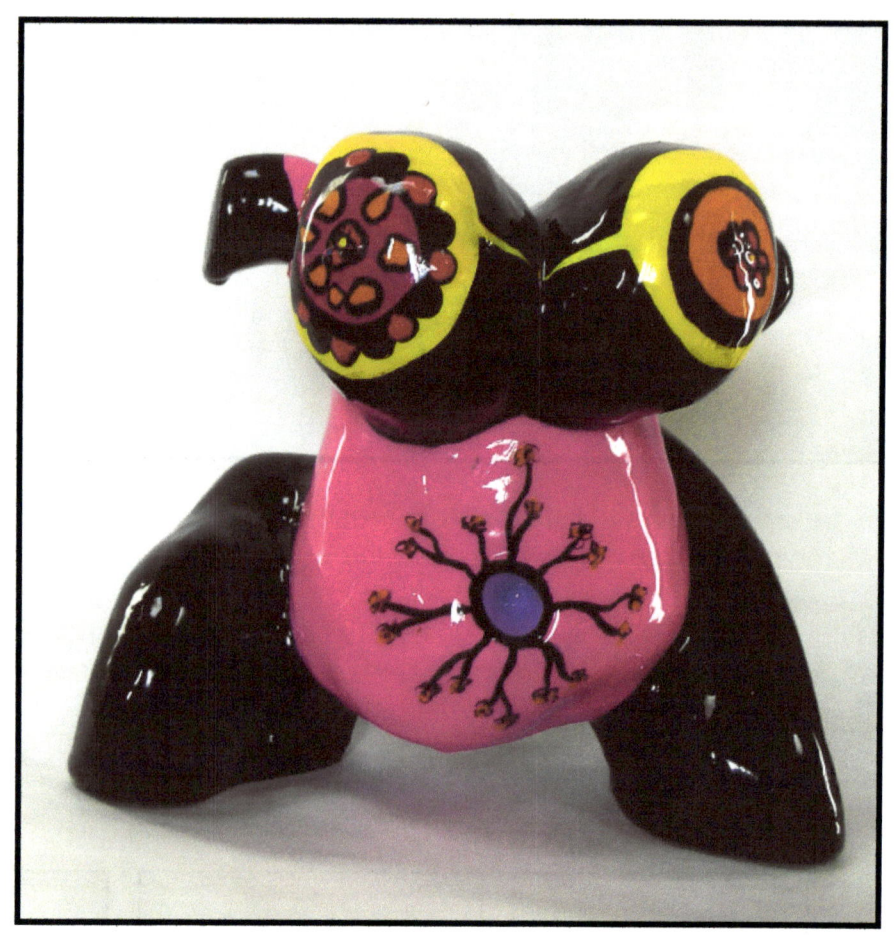

The remainder of 2005 would be spent on a vibrant collection of voluptuous throbbing sculptures. In both size and subject matter they are akin to primitive African and Latin American ritual objects, but are no doubt contemporary explorations. Whereas the engourged human form in primitive works pays homage to either the prosperity by which they have been nourished, or to their own fertile creative powers, Silva's pieces speak primarily of the sexual. Without question he alludes to fertility in gestures such as fields of flowers that grow from certain belly buttons, but the overarching feel is that of sexual celebration, of hunger for bodily and earthly delights. Breasts are

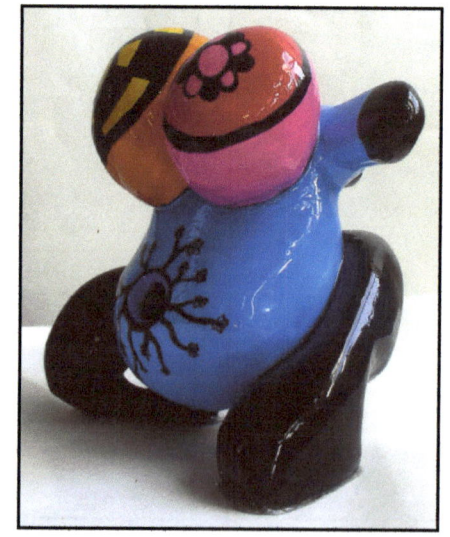

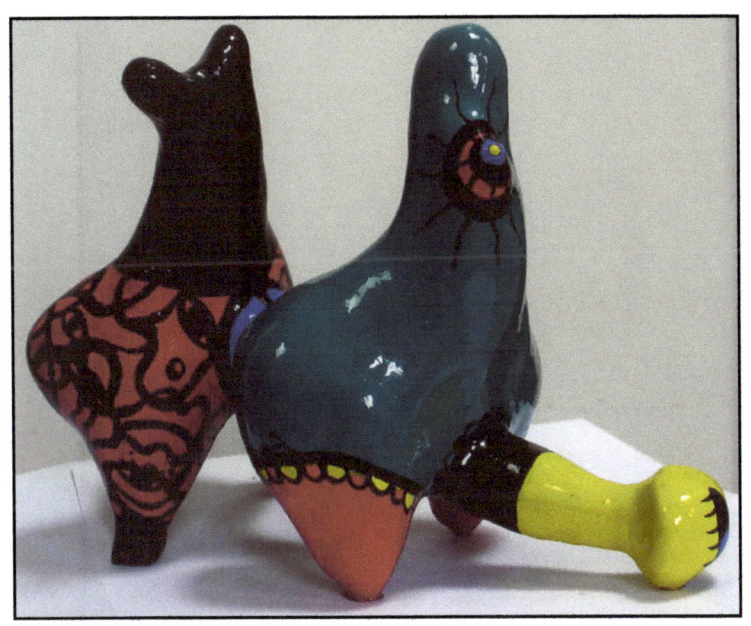

adorned with dizzying designs, laced with delicate tapestries, while the head, the arms, and for all intense purposes, the legs are left out completely. *Fuck Buddies* stands upright only because of an elongated anchoring penis (whose pleasures are the very heart of the piece). Another example of Silva's adept handling of our contemporary fascinations with the sexualized form appears in the tall, thin female, *Brazilian Woman.* On her otherwise unassuming, armless body all of her sexual possibilities call out for attention. Her legs, in tall wanton boots, extend disproportionately up to her plump buttocks; her breasts as well, ornamented, over-sized and shaped as if to hook on-lookers; all of this under her large batting eyes, her desirous smile. Through her and her accompanying idols, Silva's investigation of Brazil's sexual comodification begins in earnest.

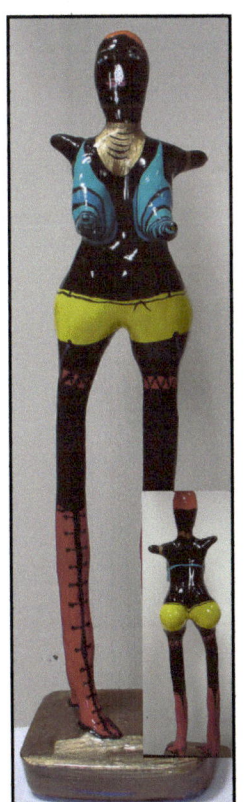

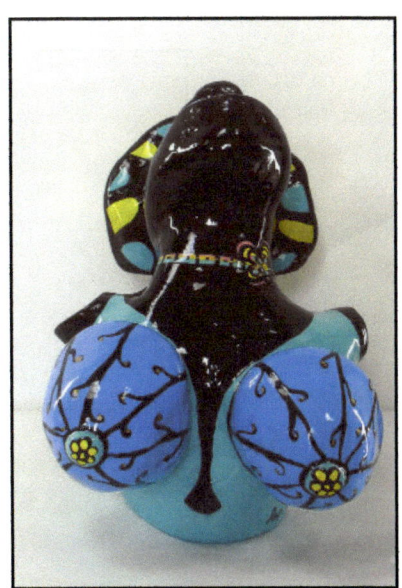

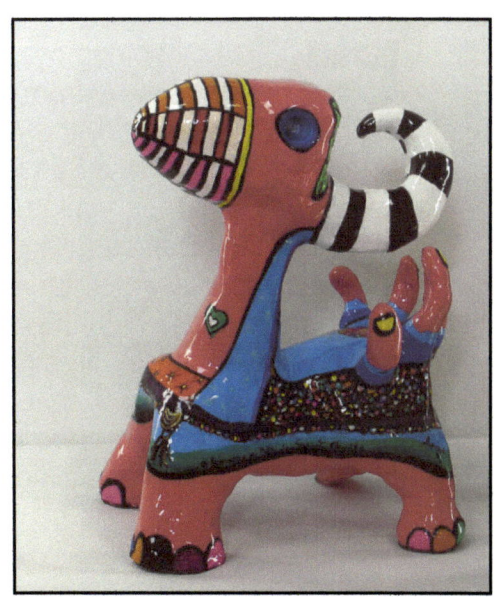

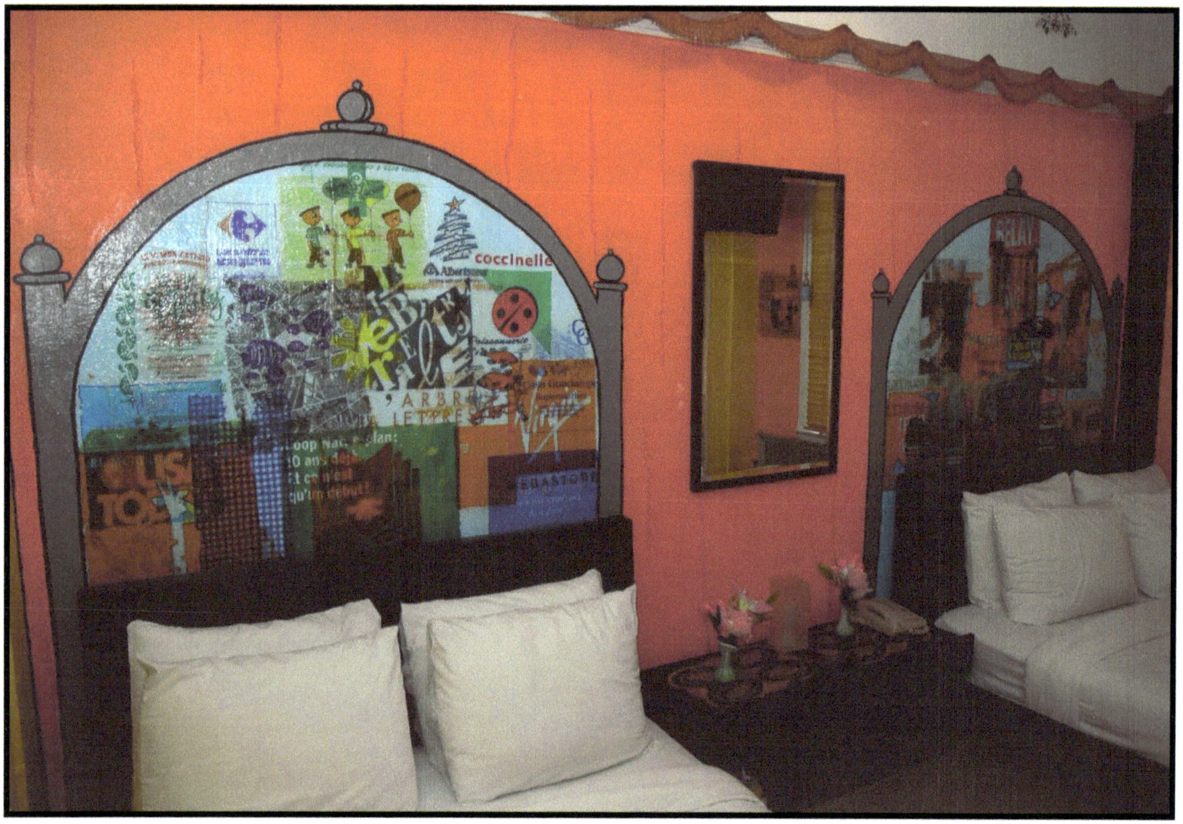

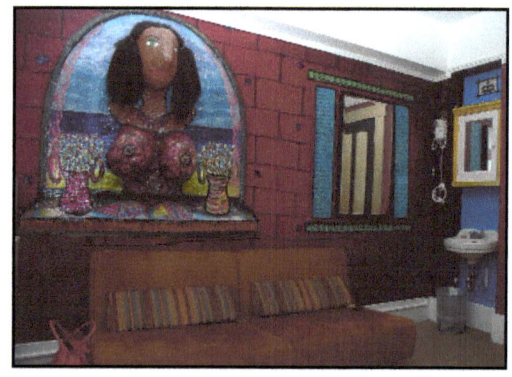

But first, two inspiring projects in 2006 would pull the artist away from this vein of work, if only for a year.   First, the commission for the Hotel Des Arts suite in San Francisco, and then a glorious outdoor sculpture in Costa Rica, would finally manifest the dexterous power of Silva's work. Having invited the artist, Bloum, to collaborate with him on the hotel suite, Silva set out to rupture the static expectations of guest quarters by creating a space where one could relax and forget they were actually inside. No surface – save for the ceiling and floor – went untouched. No media unused. From mural to sculpture, fabric to acrylics, the Regis and Bloum Suite exists as a joyous point of departure for the senses.

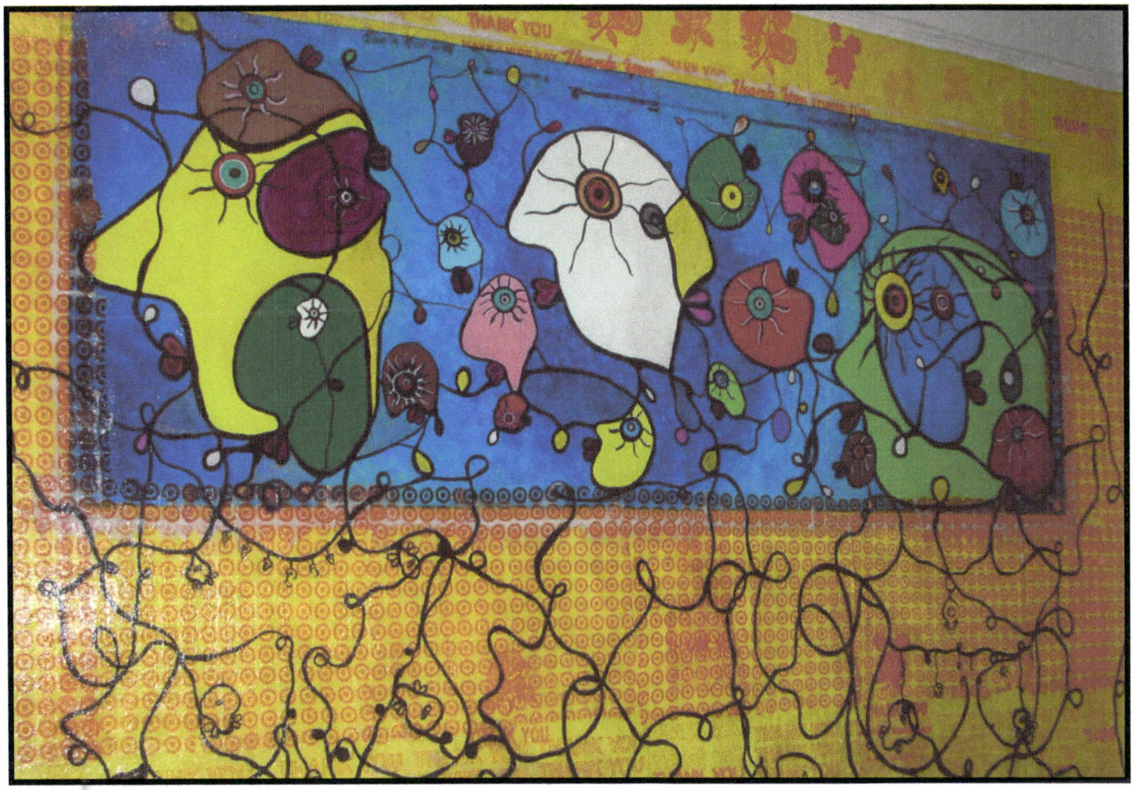

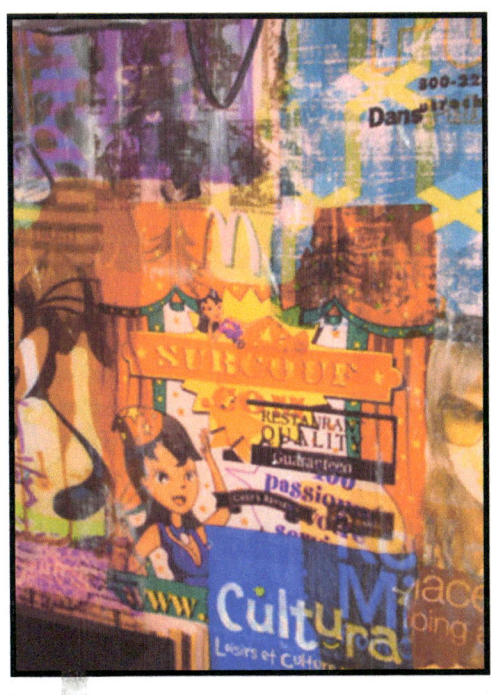

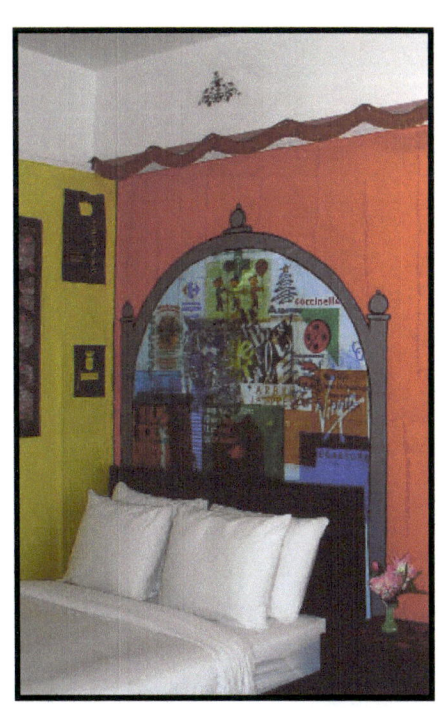

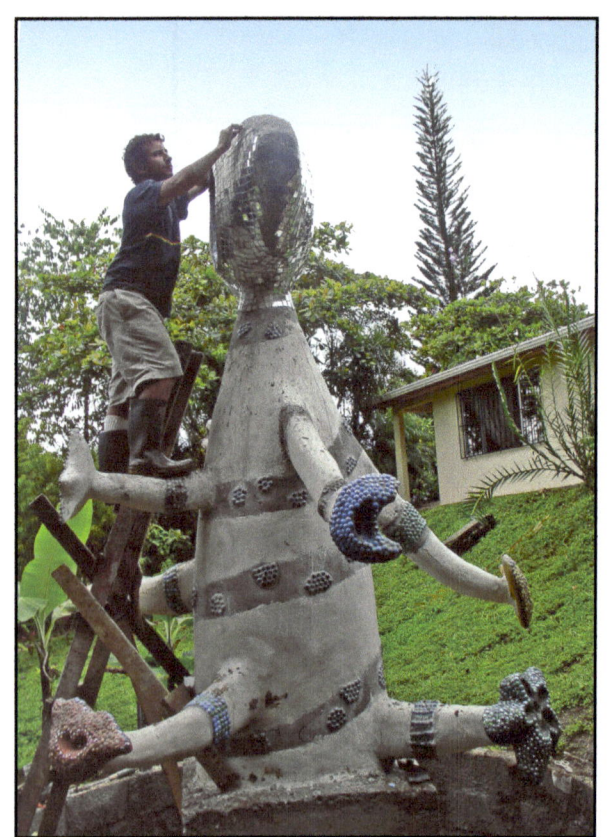

The Rains welcomed Silva to Costa Rica. Starting some mornings by 6 am, they would go on throughout the day, throughout the week even, feeding the abundant surrounding land. But having been summoned by a private client to produce a massive outdoor sculpture, Silva's spirits could not be dampened. The sculpture he'd proposed was, after all, a celebration of the myriad life forms that unite in creating the human experience and beyond. Water being key among them.

Working from his renderings, Silva hired a local welder and two construction workers to build out the initial form. Then, with the shadow of his bright creature realized, he began working the surface. Sculpting, painting, bringing to life the giant mosaic-ed entity. The work, *Humanetee – The Tower of Life*, stands some 4 meters tall and 3

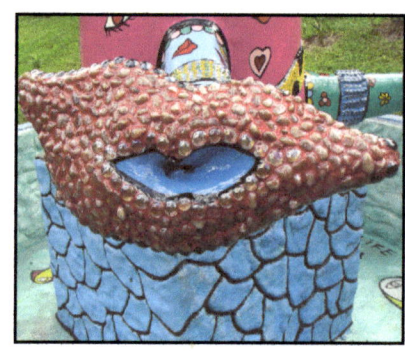

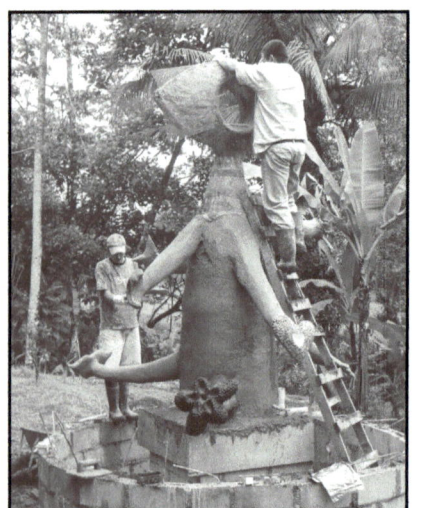

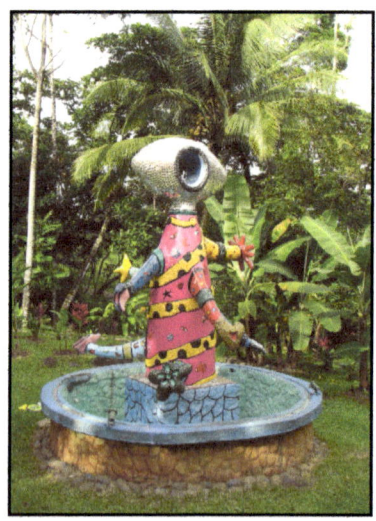

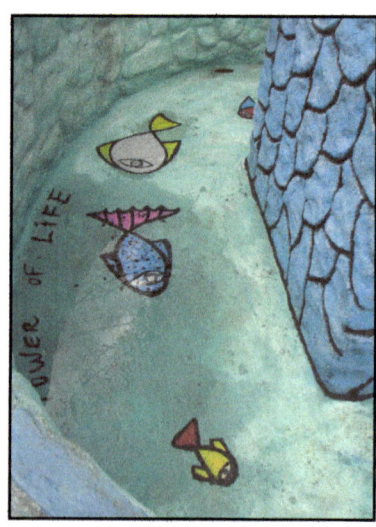

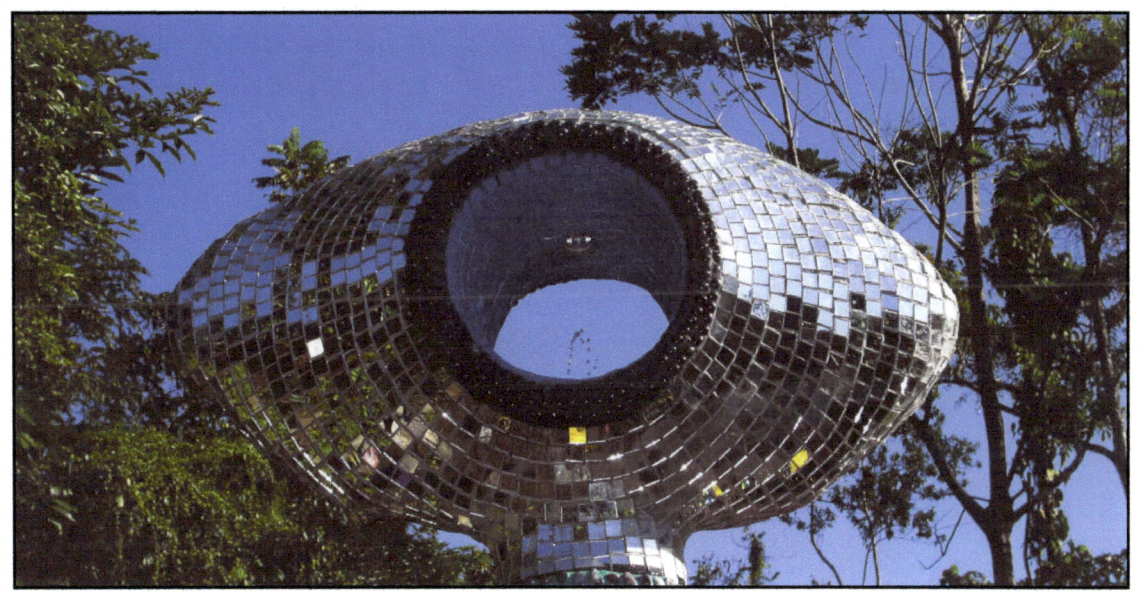

meters wide. It displays the representational sun and stars, lively flowers, the mouth, the eyes, heart and hand. All, as Silva testifies, elements which mold the human experience in this universe. The sun, which nourishes the bountiful earth; the night sky we worship; and sensually, the mouth through which we try to pronounce those ephemeral sensations we feel upon our hands, see with our eyes, and feel with our hearts. And over it all, the singular eye of the Creator, all-present and all-knowing. A masterwork.

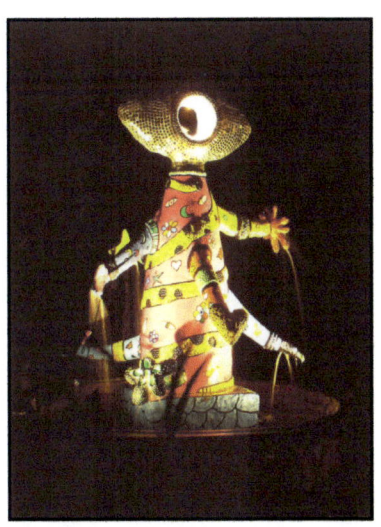

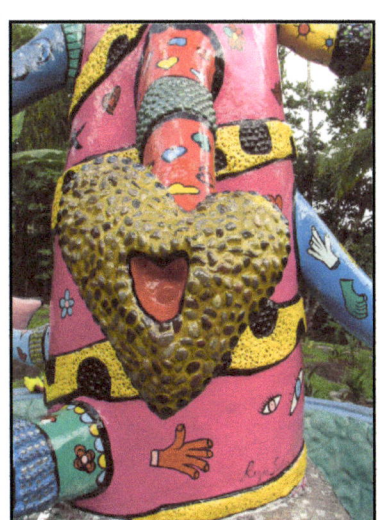

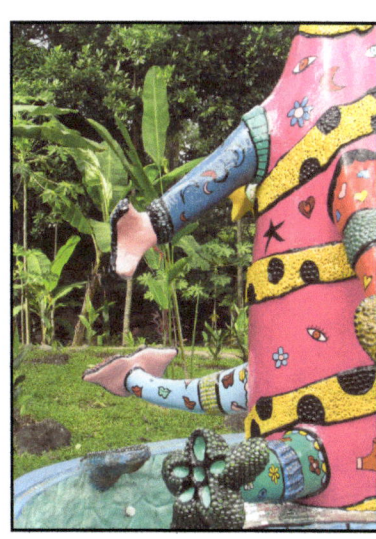

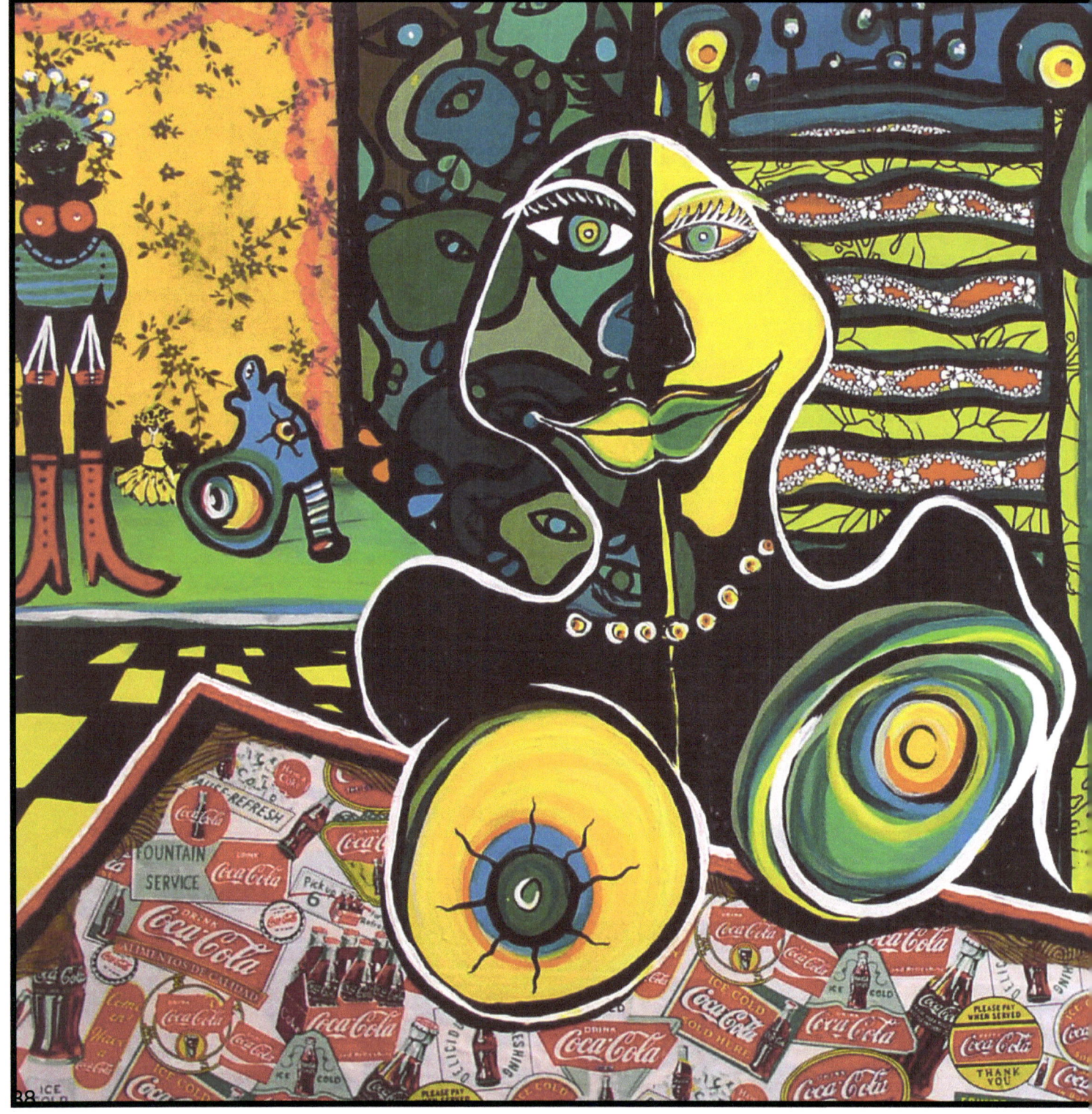

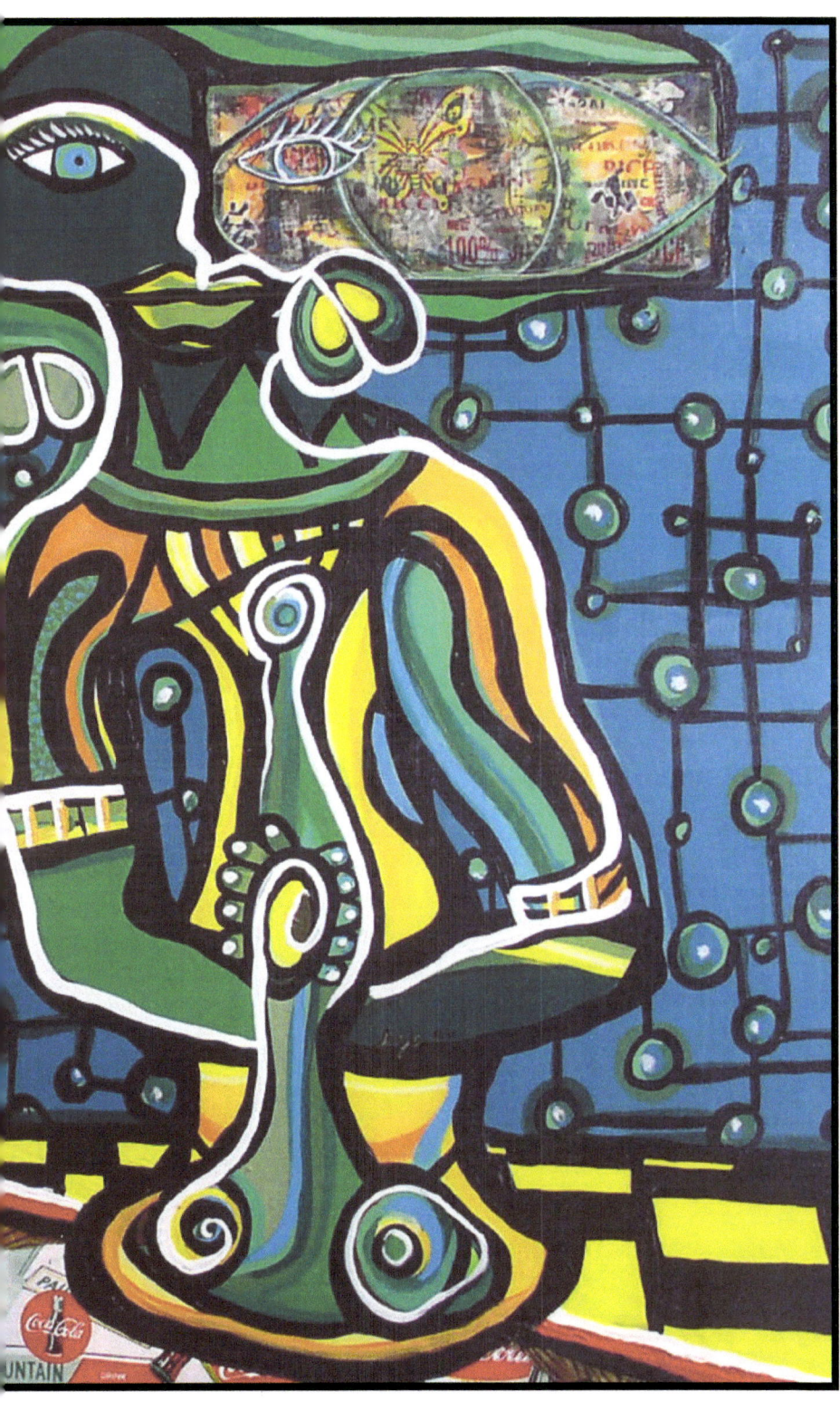

Silva's current work, his return to the canvas, is of two minds, at once lyrical and inciting. Both his narratives and abstract studies show a great deal of refinement in his employment of fabric. Stories unfold in its layering. His practice's sophistication has allowed it to move beyond wallpapering and into lucid playful gestures. His character's feelings rise from them and trail behind like aromas.

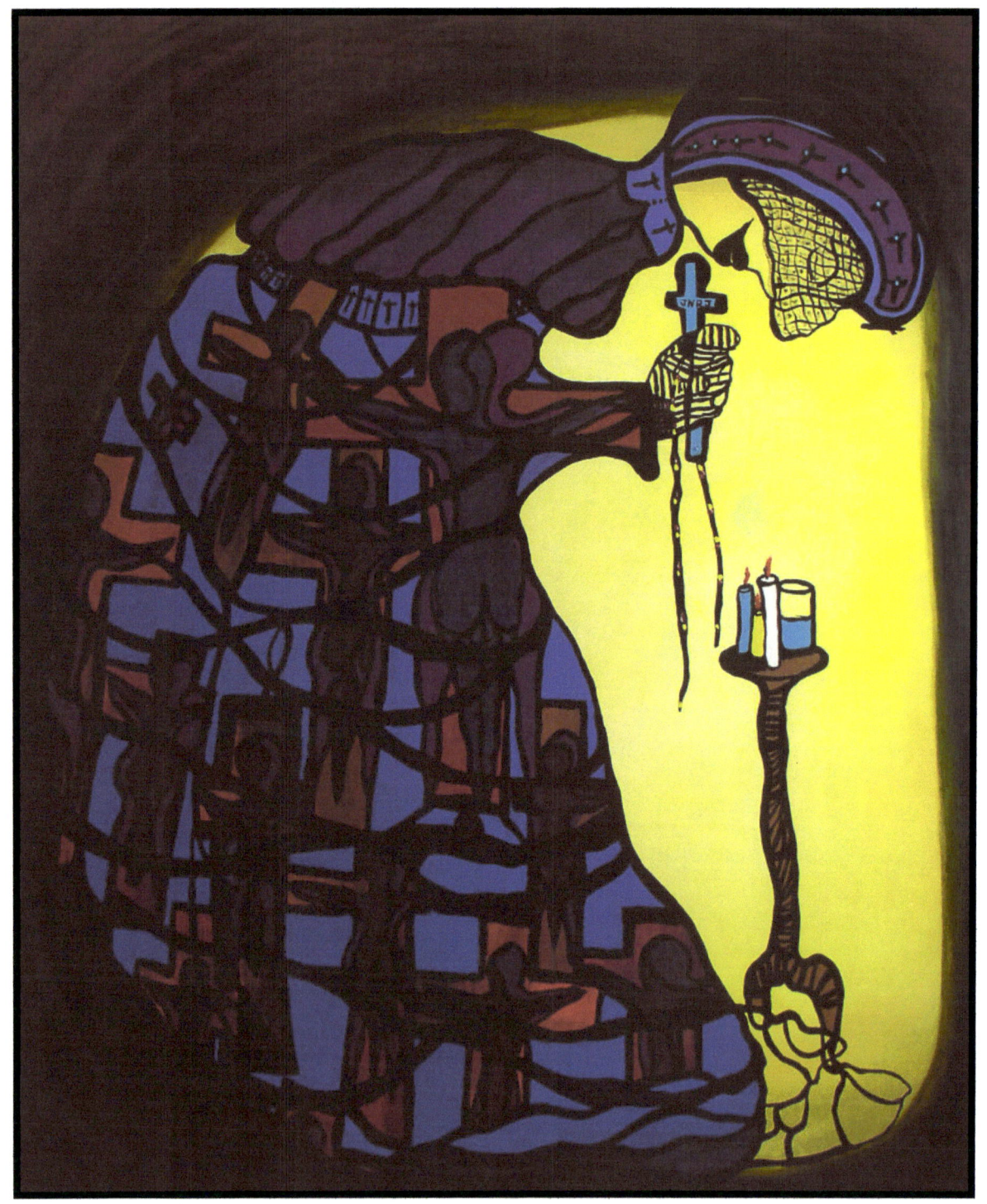

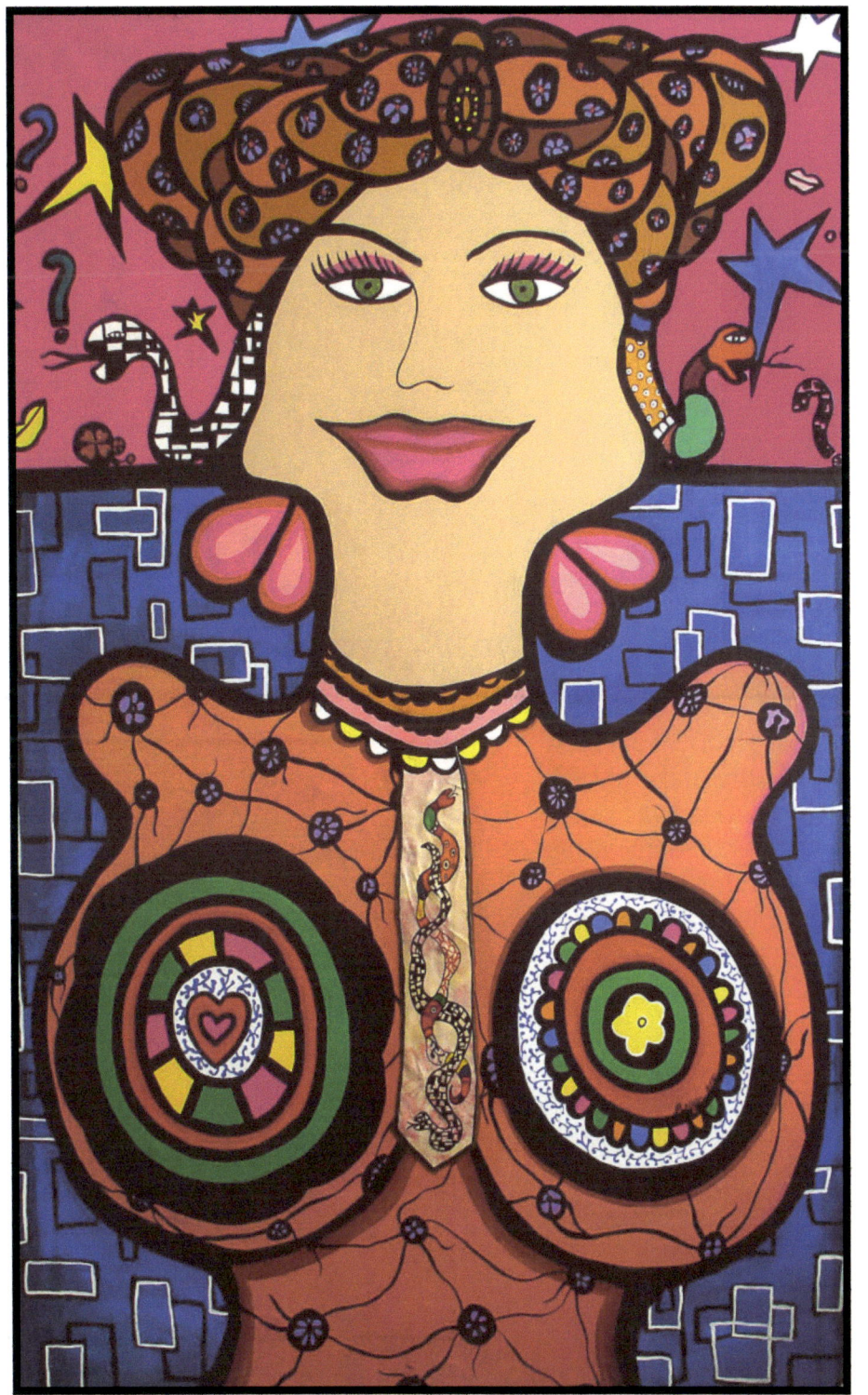

41

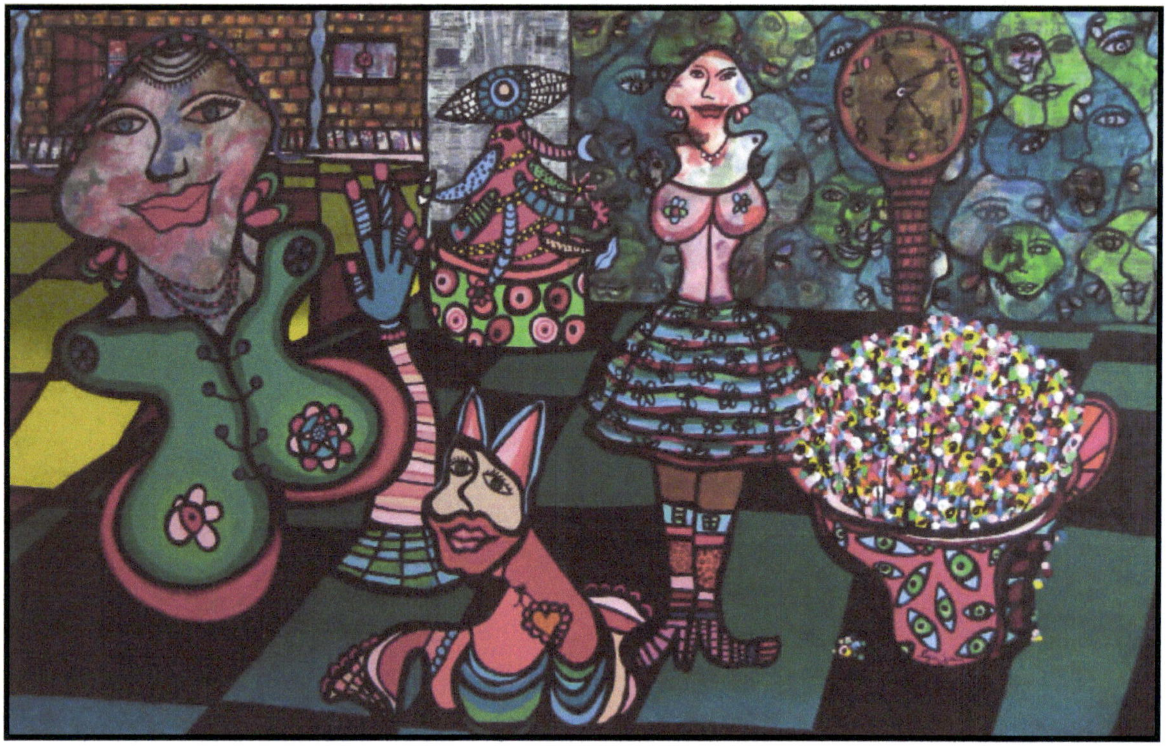

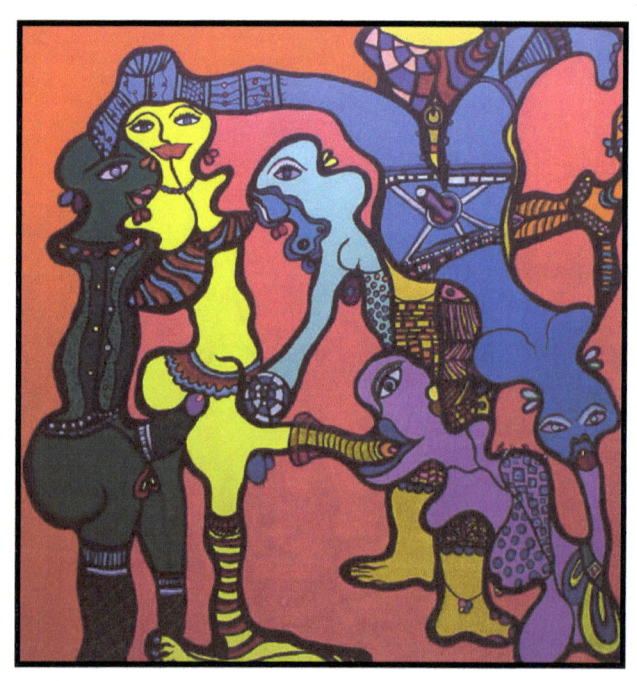

However, not all of the present work enlists the use of fabric. Silva's Carnival series is as exciting and revelational as any in his oeuvre. Depending on flat primary colors – often even monochromatic – Silva engages the complex subject of sexual salesmanship inherent to his homeland's greatest festival, Carnival. The annual festival begins forty days before Easter, marking the beginning of Lent. During Lent, Roman Catholics are commanded to abstain from all bodily pleasures. The carnival is thus celebrated as a profane farewell

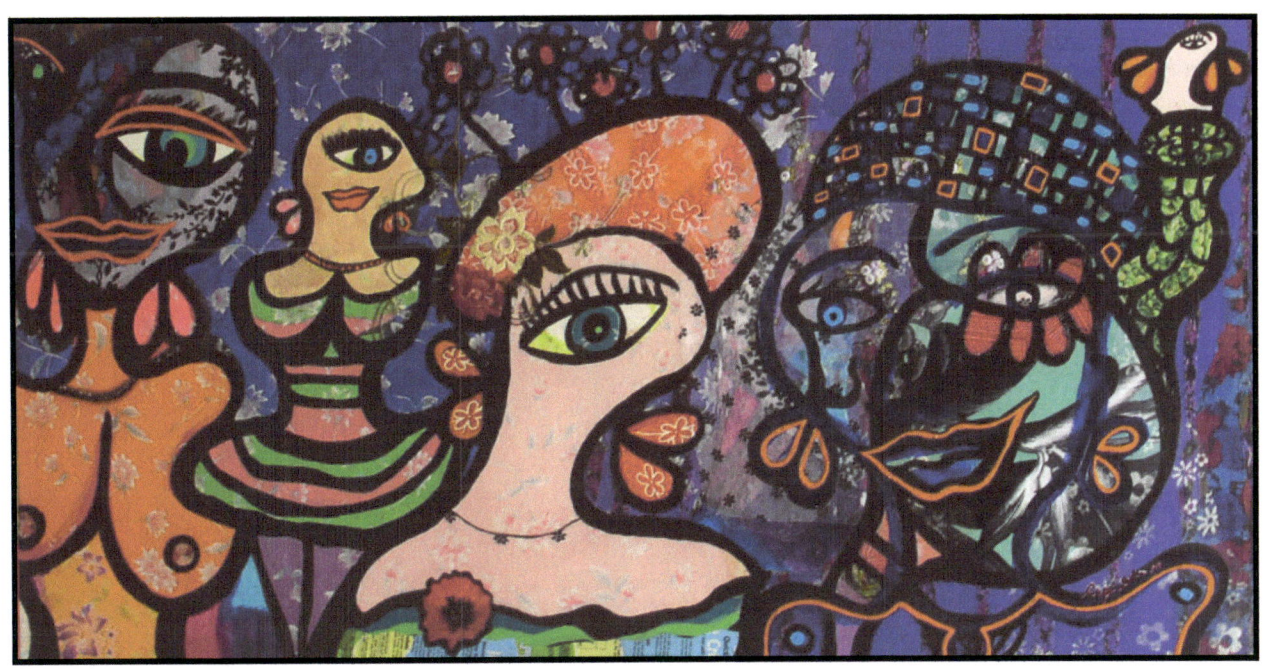

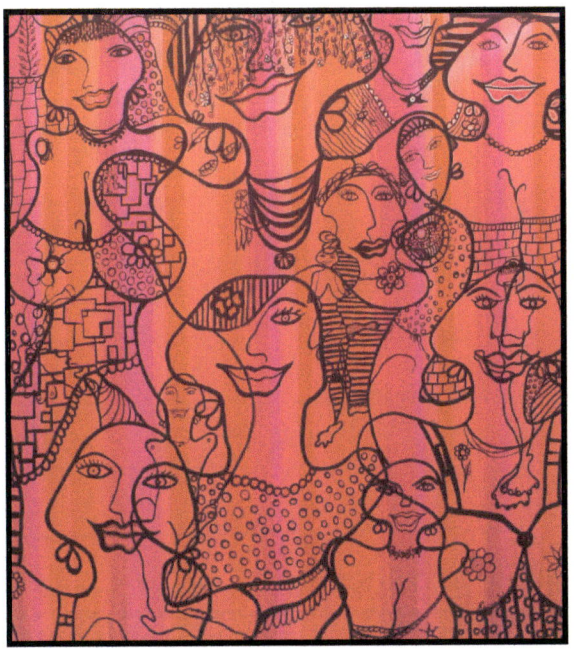

to such pleasures of the flesh. However, Silva's series does not go as far as celebrating the festival, but rather calling to the forefront the excess, the erotic overload on the senses. In The Reality Behind the Carnival six characters copulate in a flat perspective-less orgy. In Temptations the viewer is haunted by a field of female tropes. "Come to Brazil," Silva shakes his head, "We have Carnival and sex."

Luckily, there is far more to Brazil, far more to the United States, and born of these two landscapes, far more to the work of Regis Silva.

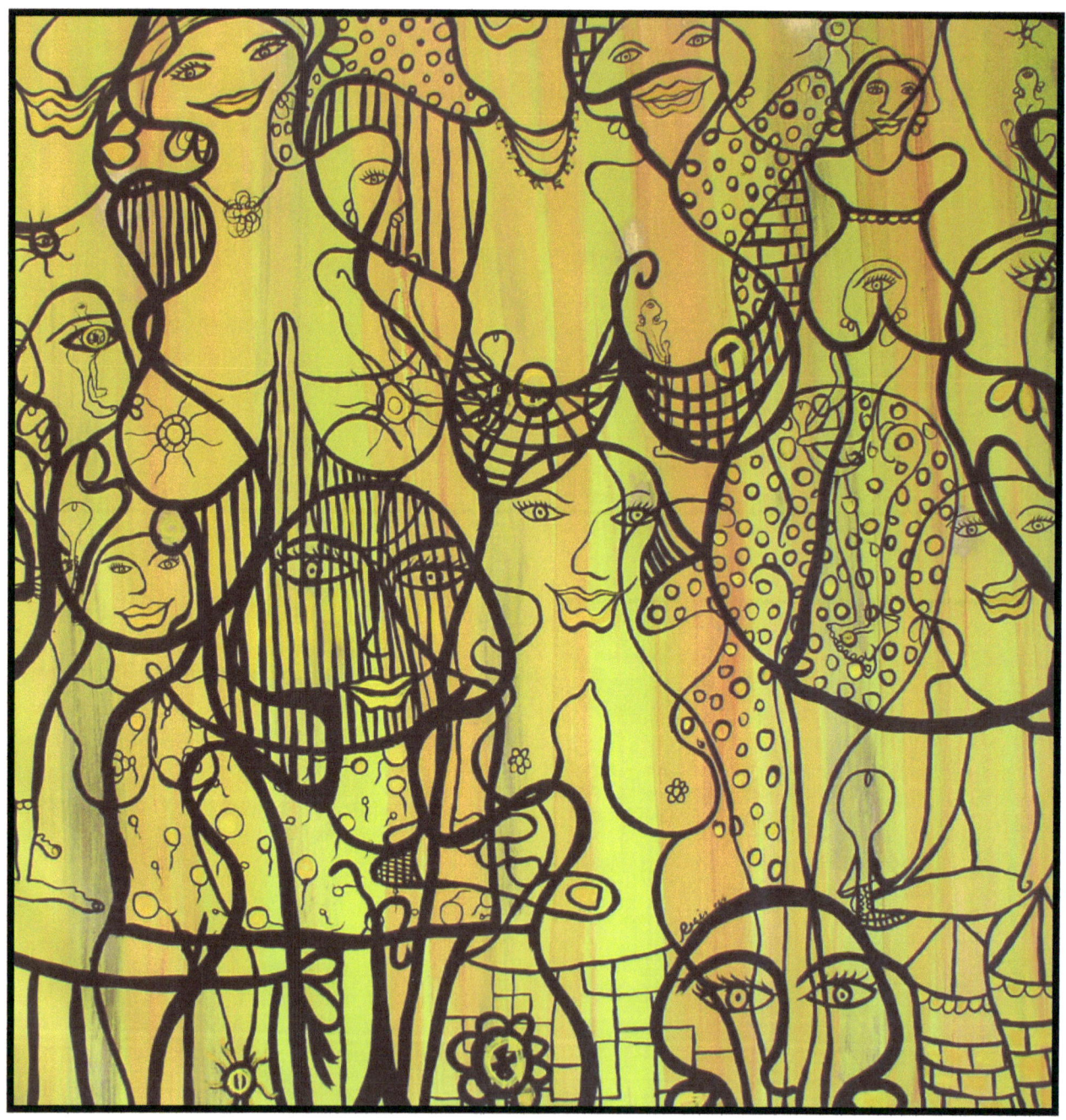

44

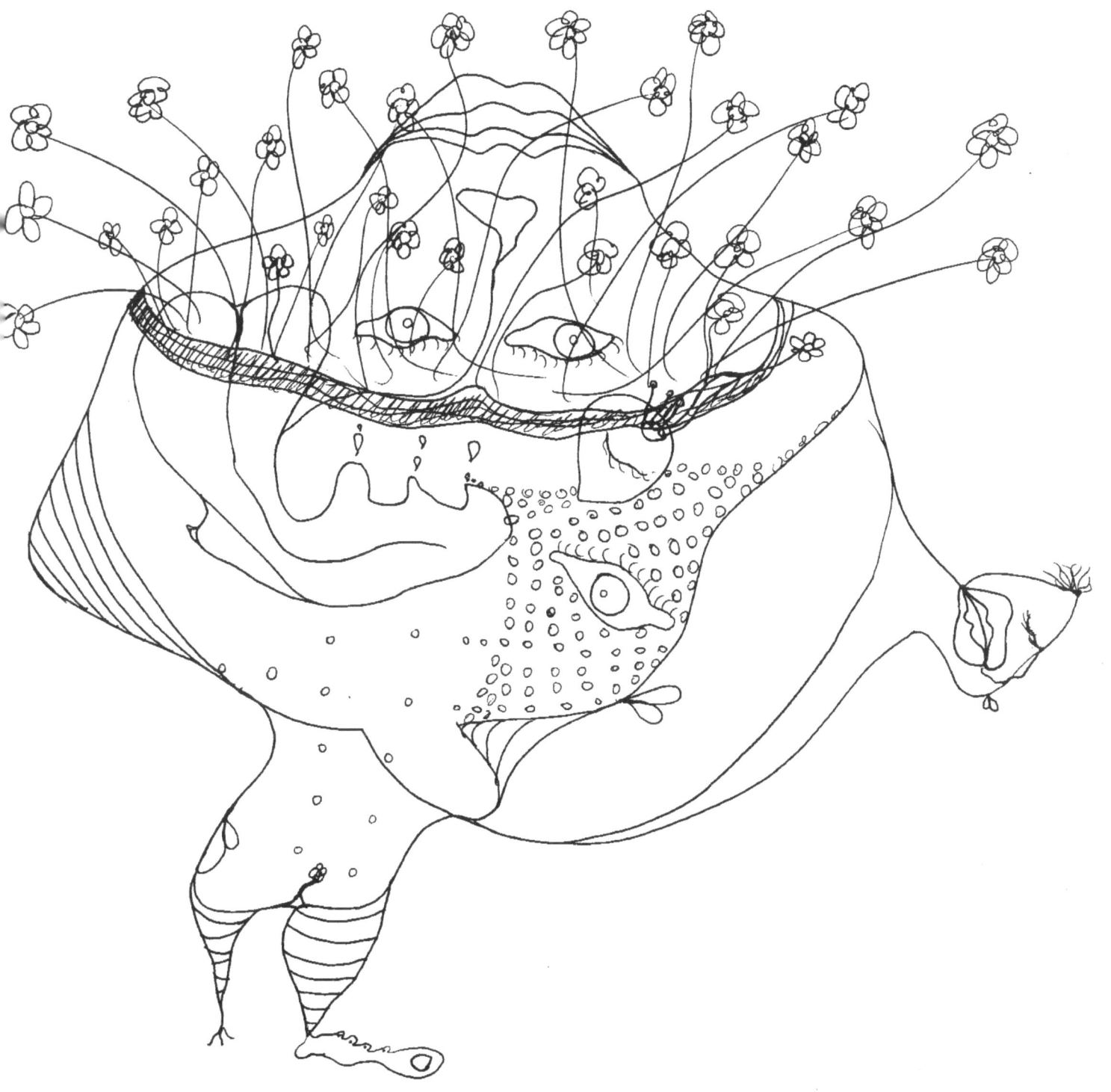

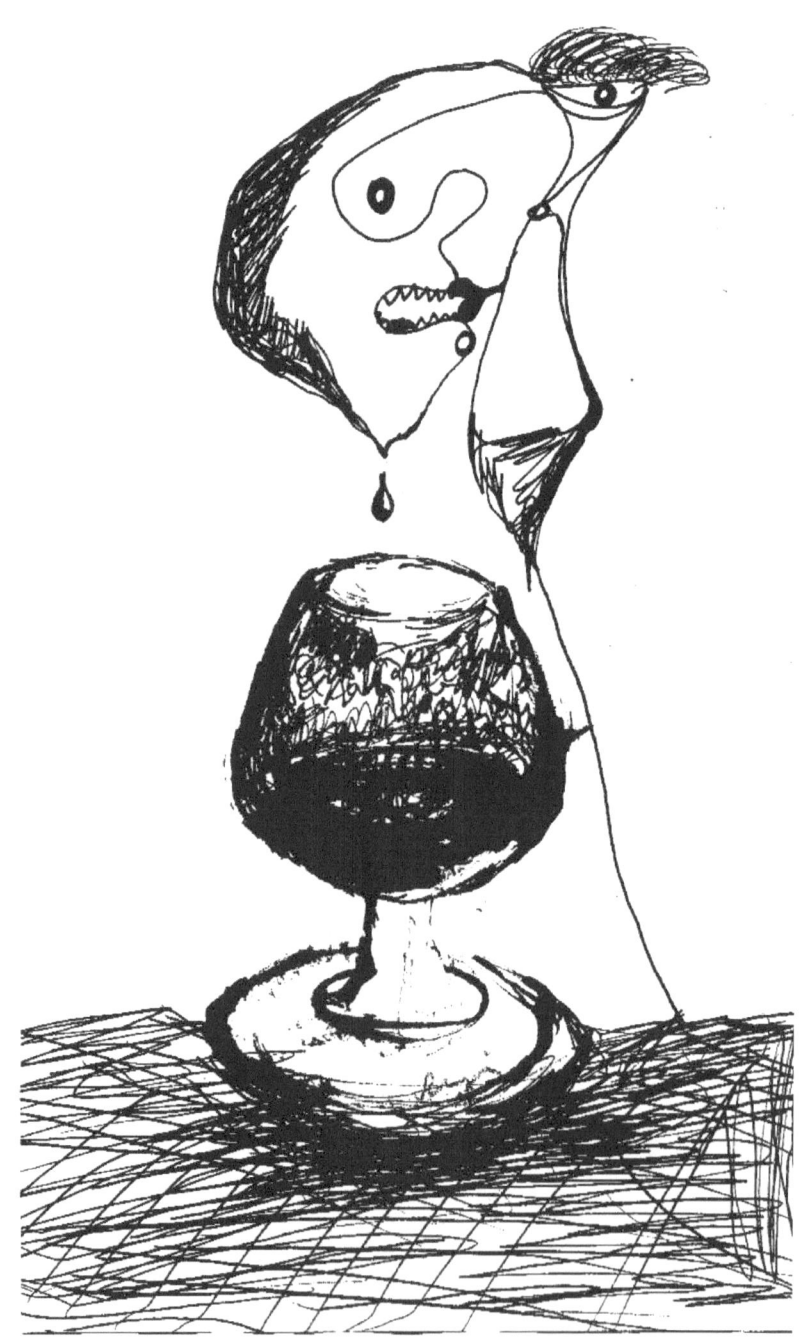

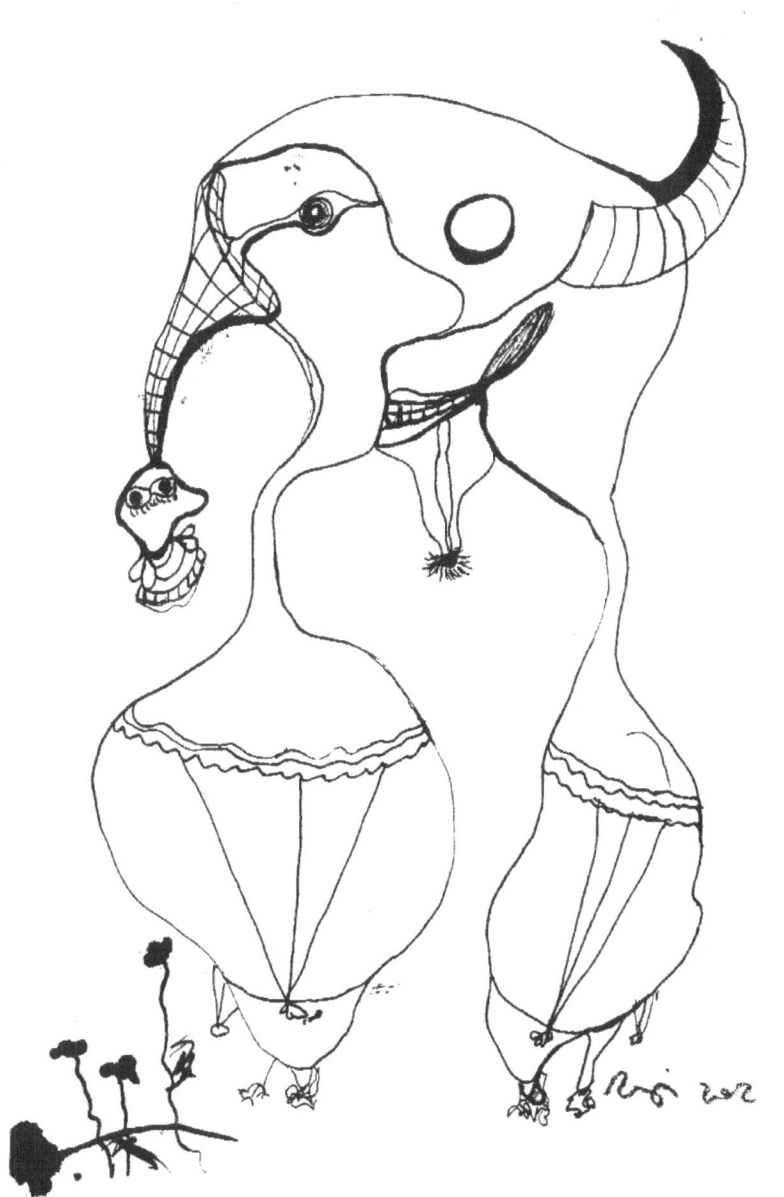

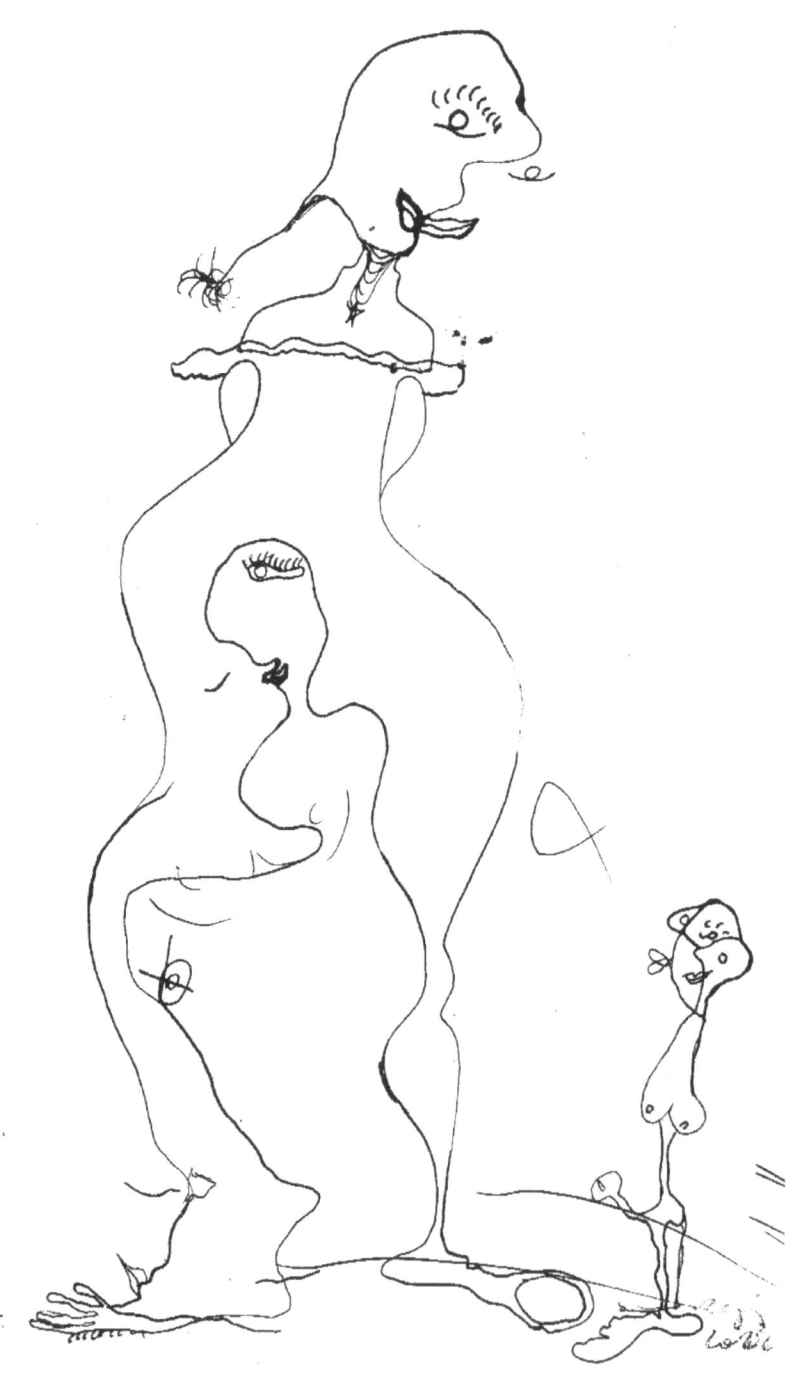

48

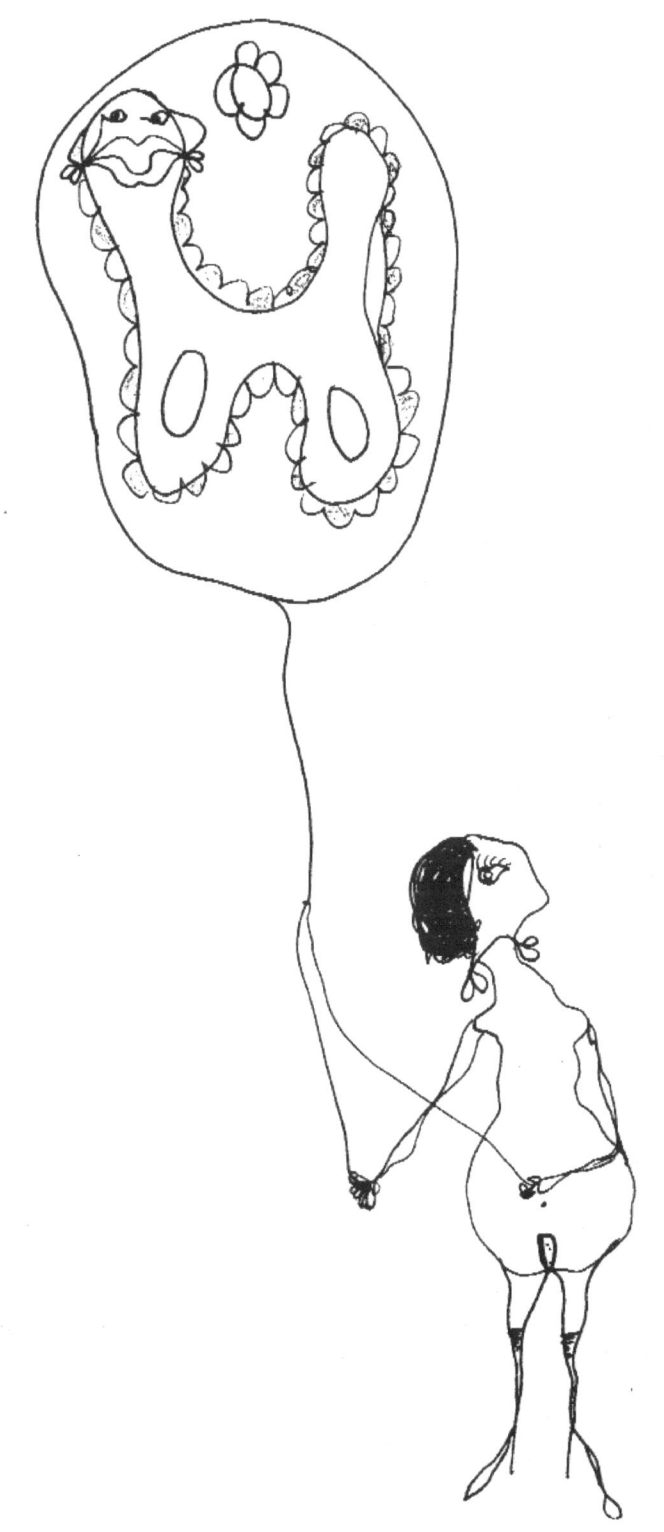

Publications

Brazzil Magazine - November 2007
BrasilBest Magazine - California, July 2007
Brasil Magazine - California, April 2007
X-Fun's Magazine - Regis & Bloum - Taiwan, 2007
Gazeta Brazilian News - Cores, Formas e Relevo com Jeitinho Brasileiro, by Leticia Kfuri - Florida, January 2005
Monterey Herald - Go! Magazine - Mixing it up - Brazilian artist Regis Silva brings an explosion of color and culture to the Pacific Grove Art Center - By Lisa Crawford Watson - California, July 2005
Monterey Conty Weekly - Brush with the Divine , by Ryan Master, California, July 2005
BrasilBest Magazine- California, July 2005
Comunidade News - by Rita Colombo, Connecticut, December 2004
Brasil Magazine - California, November 2004
City Currents Newsletter - by Patricia Arack , California, December 2004
The Brazilian Post - Tampa Bay - Florida, December 2004
Brazil Explore Magazine - by Andre Walcemberg, California, October 2004
Brasil California Magazine - California, August 2004
BrasilBest Magazine - California, Jannuary 2004
Fullerton News Tribune - California, July 2003
BrasilBest Magazine - California, August 2003
BrasilBest Magazine - California, March 2002
Orange County Register - California, August 2003
BrasilBest Magazine - California, June 2001

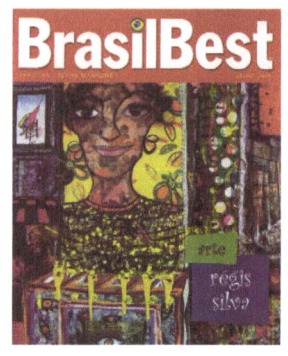

Exhibitions

Pacific Grove Art Center- Pacific Grove, CA - April, 2008
San Francisco Open Studio - San Francisco, CA - October, 2007
Museum of Art and History - Santa Cruz, CA - October/November, 2005
Pajaro Valley Art Center Gallery - Watsonville, CA - October/December 2005
Pacific Grove Art Center - Pacific Grove, CA - July/August, 2005
Blue Room Gallery - San Francisco, CA - December/January, 2004
BCC – Brazil Cultural Center -San Francisco, CA - December/January, 2003
San Francisco Open Studio San Francisco, CA - September, 2003
Muckenthaler Cultural Center -Orange County, CA - July/October, 2003
San Francisco Open Studio -San Francisco, CA - September, 2002
Everything is Art gallery -San Francisco, CA - October/January, 2002

Regis Silva

www.regissilva.com
info@regissilva.com
San Francisco, CA

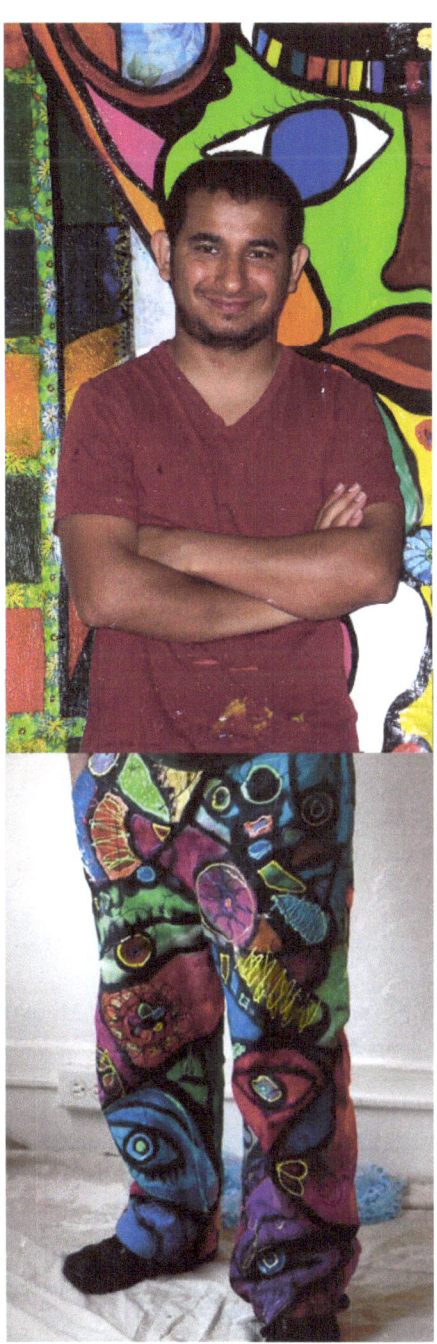

Artwork Information

Page 5 - O Outro Lado da Pomba Gira - Mixed Media - 48"W x 62"H x 14"D -2003
page 7 - City People - Acrylic - 24"Wx30"H - 2000
page 8 top - Faces - Acrylic - 24"H x 36"W - 2000
page 8 bottom - Mark's - Acrylic - 36"H x 48"W - 2000
page 9 top - Olhos de Fomes - Acrylic - 24"H x 36"W - 2004
page 9 bottom right - Heart and Veins - Acrylic - 12"H x 14"W - 2006
page 9 bottom center - Floating - 11"H x 14"W - 2004
page 9 bottom left - Waisting - 9"W x 11"H - 2004
page 10 top - High Moments - Watercolor - 18"H x 24" W - 2002
page 10 bottom - Prostitute at Mission Street - Watercolor -18"W x 24W" -2002
page 11 top - Pregant Woman -Watercolor -18"H x 24W" -2002
page 11 bottom - Memories - Watercolor -18"H x 24W" -2002
page 12 top - Friends - Watercolor 18"H x 24W" - 2002
page 12 bottom right - Neilian - Watercolor - 8"W x 15"H - 2002
page 12 bottom left - Mine -Watercolor - 18"H x 24W" -2002
page 13 - Afros at the Beach- Watercolor -8"W x 14H" -2002
page 14 top - My other dead happy dog - Watercolor - 18"H x 24W" -2002
page 15 top - The Poor Widow -Watercolor - 18"H x 24W" -2002
page 15 bottom right - The Visit - Watercolor - 12" x 18" - 2002
page 15 bottom left - The Player - Watercolor - 18"H x 24W"- 2002
page 16,17 - A Tearful Hug - Watercolor - 18" x 24" - 2002
page 18 - Oxum - Sculpture - 10"W x 18"H - 2004
page 19 top - Exu - Sculpture - 11"W x 21"H - 2004
page 19 bottom right - Iansa - Sculpture - 10"W x 18"H - 2004
page 19 bottom center - Nana Buruque - Sculpture - 10"W x 18"H - 2004
page 19 bottom left - Oxumare - Sculpture - 12"W x 28"H - 2004
page 20 - Maria Mulambeira- Acrylic/Mixed Media - 60"H x 40"W x 11"D - 2002
page 21 - Escandalo - Acrylic/Mixed Media -24"H x 26W -2005
page 22,23 - Self Portrait -Acrylic/Mixed Media - 36"W x 48" -2003
page 24 top - Pomba Gira - Mixed Media 2004 - 24"W x 38"H x 12"D
page 25 - Woman by the Window - Mixed Media - 82"H x 40"W x 12"D -2003
page 26 - Serena -Mixed Media -48"W x 124"H x 13"D -2003
page 27 - Pomba Gira Mulambo - Mixed Media, 48"W x 62"H x 14"D, 2004
page 28 top - The Bag Lady - 36"W x 48"H - Acrylic - 2006
page 28 bottom right - Lembrancas de Casa - Mixed Media -40"Wx40"H-2003
page 28 bottom left - Twins - Acrylic/Mixed Media -45"W x 50"H -2003
page 29 top - Filhos de Indios - Acrylic/Mixed Media -24"H x 26W -2006
page 29 bottom right - Leaving you - Acrylic/Mixed Media - 12"H x 16W -2004
page 29 bottom left - Sadness - Acrylic/Mixed Media -14"H x 10W -2004
page 30,31 top - Fabric paint - 10 yards - 2005

page 30 bottom - Naked Body Paint - Model: Cristiane Viana, San Francisco Street Carnival 2005
page 31 - Dress made with fabric paint - Dandara - Singer for art opening 2005
page 32 top - Pink Breast Woman - Sculpture -2006
page 32 bottom - Blue Breast Woman -Sculpture-2006
Page 33 top - Fuck Buddies -Sculpture -2006
page 33 bottom right - Celestial Horse -Sculpture -2006
page 33 bottom center - Woman with Chapeu -Sculpture -2006
page 33 bottom left - Brazilian Woman -Sculpture -2006
page 34,35 - Mural inside Hotel des Arts Regis & Bloum suite - 500/501- 2006
page 34 top - Wall painted by Regis & Bloum, Hotel des Arts
page 34 bottom right - Wall painted by Regis, Hotel des Arts
page 34 bottom left - Regis working on the mural, Hotel des Arts
page 35 top - Wall painted by Regis & Bloum, Hotel des Arts
page 35 bottom right - Wall painted by Bloum, Hotel des Arts
page 35 bottom left - Wall painted by Regis & Bloum, Hotel des Arts
page 36,37 - Humanetee - The tower of Life - Sculpture, 15'H x 10'W, Costa Rica - 2006
page 38,39 - The Eating Room - Mixed Media - 32"H x 44"W - 2006
page 40 - Praying in Vain -Acrylic - 48"H x 36"W - 2006
page 41 - Niki - Acrylic - 60"H x 48"W - 2007
page 42 top - Drawing Objects - 36"W x 24"H Acrylic 2007
page 42 bottom - The Reality Behind Carnaval - 50"W x 50"H - Acrylic - 2007
page 43 top - Behind the Scenes - 60"H x 48"W Acrylic - 2007
page 43 bottom - Gossip - 38"W x 26"H - Acrylic - 2007
page 44 - Temptation - 50"W x 50"H - Acrylic -2007
page 45 - A Lavadeira de Ropa - Drawing - 6"W x 8"H - 2005
page 46 - O Vicio - Drawing - 5"W x 6"H - 2002
page 47 - Infidel - Drawing - 4"W x 7"H - 2002
page 48 - I Have a Surprise for you - Drawing - 5"W x 8"H - 2003
page 49 - Playing alone - Drawing - 5"W x 8"H - 2002
page 51 - Regis Silva

www.ingramcontent.com/pod-product-compliance
Lightning Source LLC
Chambersburg PA
CBHW051053180526
45172CB00002B/623